ONE DAY *Closer*

Strength for the Seasons of Life

Volume 2

6 Weeks of Meditations
for Traumatic Times

Dr. William H. Curtis

One Day Closer: Strength for the Seasons of Life - Volume 2
By Dr. William H. Curtis

The Church Online, LLC
1000 Ardmore Blvd.
Pittsburgh, PA 15221

International Standard Book Number:
978-1-68548-000-4

Library of Congress Catalog Number: Available Upon Request
Printed in the United States of America

TABLE OF CONTENTS

DAY 1 MEDITATION

PERSISTENCE OF FAITH

Luke 18:1-8 frames our meditation for today:

> Jesus told them a story showing that it was necessary for them to pray consistently and never quit. He said, "There was once a judge in some city who never gave God a thought and cared nothing for people. A widow in that city kept after him: 'My rights are being violated. Protect me!'

> "He never gave her the time of day. But after this went on and on he said to himself, 'I care nothing what God thinks, even less what people think. But because this widow won't quit badgering me, I'd better do something and see that she gets justice—otherwise I'm going to end up beaten black-and-blue by her pounding.'"

Then the Master said, "Do you hear what that judge, corrupt as he is, is saying? So what makes you think God won't step in and work justice for his chosen people, who continue to cry out for help? Won't he stick up for them? I assure you, he will. He will not drag his feet. But how much of that kind of persistent faith will the Son of Man find on the earth when he returns?" (MSG).

This parable Jesus shared is intended to teach that what is at risk when Jesus returns is not a history of faith. Jesus implies that many will have surrendered to the curiosity of faith. Still, others will have flirted with the notion of wedding it to a season of their lives. But, Jesus says the threat when He returns is to find the absence of persistence among those who had a history of faith.

To teach this, Jesus suggests that this woman in the text receives the justice she demands not based on how entitled she was or how egregious the offense committed against her was. She receives justice because the judge said if he did not respond to her, then she was going to wear him down with her consistent pounding on the door. Jesus says: When the Lord returns, He will be looking not only for people who have the evidence of faith, but He will be looking for people who have the *persistence of faith.* The persistence Jesus will be looking for is an unembarrassed boldness. That is what it means in the original language. It meant this woman was not going to this judge over and over ashamed, as she passed people, or that the judge has to see her again; her boldness is without shame.

The woman in this parable did not care about how many times she had approached and been denied. The woman was more determined to get the justice she was seeking.

The Lord is looking for that special something in your life that is the bridge to the next experience in your spiritual journey. Have you surrendered to the work your spirituality is doing in you to make you the kind of person who will not be denied that certain "something"? Will you keep fighting to be heard, to walk through, and to fight what is trying to hold you back?

This is the only way to walk this season of difficulty in your life. It is the only way to push back against the resistance pushing against you. It is to climb every day, emotionally wishing for even a soft descent but determined that if the path never leads down and keeps me on this steep incline for an indefinite period of time, then I will not be denied the prize I know awaits me at the top of this hill. I want you to live with that kind of spiritual confidence–that determined drive and laser focus. Make the refrain you hear me offering your steadily rehearsed mantra: I will walk my faith with such dogged tenacity that I will not be denied the complete expression of God's imagination for my life.

I will not be denied the best that God intends for me despite the fatiguing persistence required to receive it. You will get more by living not to be denied than you ever will receive living thinking you are entitled.

George Mueller said: "It is not enough to begin to pray, nor to pray aright; nor is it enough to continue for a time to pray; but we must patiently, believingly, continue in prayer until we obtain an answer."

I want to shape this persistent image in you. When it comes to your relationship with Jesus, you have to live refusing to be denied. Keep pounding at the door of God's provisions and realize that He is not limited to what you thought it was going to be. God can show you as a reward for your persistence how wide and expansive His imagination is.

Paul Tournier, the great psychiatrist, and Christian counselor tells in one of his essays about the first time he tried to pray for a solid hour. Tournier says that he set his watch on the table and began to pray. After what he thought was a good while, Tournier checked the watch. Only ten minutes had passed. Several times he did this, struggling to stay with his prayer for an hour. Tournier said when the sixty minutes had passed, he felt nothing fatigue—no sense of blessing, no sense of relationship with God at all. Just sixty minutes of drudgery. But then, Tournier says, on a whim, he fell on his knees for one more minute—just one more minute after the sixty. In that one extra minute moment, God flooded into his life in a fresh, cleansing, and exciting way.

The hour of struggle had been the necessary prelude for that one moment of spiritual joy. I am telling you that some of us do not need a miracle or an intervention. We need persistence. Hang in there one more minute and keep pounding until something shifts.

Success on whatever level and the stage is predicated on the belief in the vision that gets you started, but it is completed by the persistence you cling to throughout. It is rewarded by God blessing you with response to your persistent prayer or effort or belief. Most people do not end up in a powerful place in life because they got a break. Most people in powerful stations in life arrived there because they refused to let *not* getting a break make them quit. If you are not slated for an easy path with no struggles and strains, then clothe yourself with persistence and announce that you are in it to not be denied.

What are you waiting for? What are you working on? What are you hoping for? What are you waiting to move past? What are you hoping to accomplish? It is going to take more than initial effort and an occasional burst of energy. It will take the persistent effort that pushes you past fatigue and that gets you up early when you want to sleep late. The kind of effort that makes you stay when others vacate. But you have to live refusing to be denied.

Tom Keller was on sentry duty during his time in the military when he fell asleep standing on his feet. Something awakened him. As Keller opened his eyes, he saw spit-shined boots directly opposite his own. Keller wanted to curse, but instead, he said, "In Jesus' name, Amen!" and looked up to face his superior officer. The superior officer, who did not like Tom, cursed. The officer was ready to bust Tom down to a lower rank. But while it was a felony—and in wartime, a capital offense—to fall asleep on sentry duty, it was no crime to pray.

So, Tom's pretend prayer kept him from getting busted down for sleeping.

I saw the most fascinating thing recently. After a storm had passed, I grabbed my laptop as I had done on previous days and started editing this meditation. I noticed a little bird with a thin twig in its beak cross the deck and go up in a four-foot tree that sits at the corner of the deck. I paid no more attention to it until later when I noticed the same little bird with what I thought was the same thin twig making the same move. Then it dawned on me that this little bird did not have the same twig but another one. I decided that since I was talking to you about persistence, I would watch that bird build. From 3 o'clock until well after 5 o'clock, this bird, by itself, grabbed and pulled thin twigs and went up that tree. I thought, "God, thank You for the visual demonstration." You build whatever you need to advance your life not only if you believe but if you persist, one thin effort at a time. The big door opens for you in life when you move past the obstacles in a way that helps you build your nest and not allow it to make you trash your dreams.

Don't get weary in doing well, my friend. I would not mind at all if God thought, "Let me bless Pastor Curtis because if I don't answer his prayers, he is going to trouble Me in prayer until I do." I would not be ashamed to walk around with the blessing I possess because I would not be denied.

Don't be denied; be persistent. Your happiness, your freedom, your capacity, your project completion, and your elevation are all tied not just to your effort but to your persistence. What about your life? What do you want for your life that is calling not for your affirmation of desire but for your intention to be persistent until God says something about it, grants it or expresses His denial of it? The pearl of the great price today is that God will not mind at all if you talk to Him about the same thing day and night, because there is so much spiritual potential in you just talking to Him.

QUESTIONS FOR THOUGHT

1. What would you ask God for if you knew you would not be denied?

2. Does God ever get tired of hearing from you?

3. Are you one to give up quickly or easily, or do you have the tenacity of spirit?

LET US PRAY

Lord, I pray that we would affirm in our lives the need to be like the woman who would not give up on what she could only get from that judge. We know You have plans for us and we want to see them fulfilled. We know You want to use us, and we want our gifts and graces matured to the level that matches the work You have assigned to our hands. We will not be denied from experiencing the complete joy that comes with knowing You.

We still our hands, focus our vision, arrest our thoughts, and change our minds to live determined not to be denied the imaginings You have concerning our lives. Thank You for responding to our persistent knock, repeated prayers, and constant approaches to Your throne. We only have You to go to and we keep coming because we know only You have exactly what we need. May we have a great day full of discoveries about Your goodness and will for our lives. We ask it in Jesus' name. Amen.

DAY 2 MEDITATION

ACCESS THROUGH GOD

Romans chapter 5 is a powerful explanation of God's plan for humanity's salvation. God, possessing all knowledge-meaning there is no knowledge that has not always been known to God, nor could there ever be-when Adam and Eve were created, knew that the riskiest part of creating them was giving them free choice. God also knew that goodness is only its best expression when tempted by its counter. So God's plan for our salvation and redemption was imagined at the same time we were created. The sin Adam and Eve committed in the Garden was not only expected but was also eternally met by the release of God's plan for dealing with human estrangement from Him.

Paul wrote Romans 5 to address the theological misunderstanding that existed in the early church in Rome regarding sin, the law, and salvation. Paul explained how it all came into being. The first part of Paul's explanation was to suggest that God created the law so that humanity would know it transgressed God's law. If there had been no original sin, then there would be no need for the law because the relationship we have with God would have no transgressions to bring distance and injury to that relationship.

For example, if every single person always drove the speed limit, then there would be no need to post speed limit signs. We have speed limit signs and highway patrol because there is in our driving nature the inherent want to exceed the limit and to be thrilled by it. The same holds true with sin. We were given the law for one reason—not to correct our behavior, because the law cannot do that. Only our love for God can do that. The law was given to us to reveal how we have transgressed God's law. The law makes us aware of how we have drifted from the plan God has for us to enjoy Him forever.

Paul teaches that there was needed another part of this plan, which was payment for sin through death. It is simple why death is required: because in Adam's original sin we were introduced to death and in Jesus, that penalty is covered and paid. Since we carry this seed of death, we are not able to pay that penalty for ourselves. Jesus, the sinless one, would purchase us back, giving us a chance to live in the right relationship with God. We call this redemption. The only way to do this completely was for Jesus to die in our place. Now, the sin that is ours to pay for, Jesus paid for us, and that makes us "justified," which simply means we are declared righteous again. All of this was imagined before God even said, "Let there be..."

Against that brief history, I want you now to hear Paul in Romans 5:1-2:

> **Therefore, having been justified by faith, we have peace with God through our Lord Jesus Christ, through whom also we have access by faith into this grace in which we stand, and rejoice in hope of the glory of God. (NKJV).**

Let us extract just one portion of what Paul says: "We have access by faith into this grace in which we stand." You stand in a grace provided by God, which is to have been a part of God's eternal plan. That plan includes your life being justified by the obedient work of Christ to purchase the opportunity for you to live in an unbreachable relationship with God. If God would go through all of this to make sure that you have no separation from Him when it comes to spiritual and eternal matters, then does it not stand to reason that God would intend the same when it comes to temporal matters as well?

I do not know what dominates one side of the scale that makes you feel perhaps like you are locked out of or denied or made to struggle harder to access a life that gives you a sense of purpose or joy or fulfillment. While you might feel distant and maybe even locked out from these realities, your walk with Christ certainly has provided you access. This access should shape everything from your vision to your emotions. *Access* in the Greek is simply understood as admission. You have free admission into the grace of God for everything that makes up your life.

I have been granted entrance and admission into a lot of meetings that while sitting there I have wondered why they were ever convened because of their lack of focus, content, or intention. The excitement or anticipation of having been admitted was quickly dissipated by the anemic agenda that greeted me. But when Paul talks about access, he means that you are granted admission into something that he calls grace-and it is no doubt exciting to have simply been admitted. But it is all the more exciting to realize what you are admitted into.

You are admitted into a grace that reveals total eradication of everything that denied you a clear opportunity to move towards the life God purposed for you. The interruptions and demands, the pressures and weights you carry—all are assumed in this access granted to you. So do not accept admittance into the grace God extends for this new day carrying the weights that make you think it has nothing great in store for you.

With the access comes the lifting of everything that would deny you a clear opportunity to move so much closer to the will of God for your life. How does that thought infuse your energy, lift your spirit, or ignite your drive? What does it do to change your mood and encourage your mind to know that God is giving you access so He can grace you with a chance to redefine every responsibility you have this week without the weight of last week's interpretation? It may have been a weight last week, but this week, having taken advantage of the access graced to me, it is a blessing to be able to do the same thing I called a burden last week. Understanding and taking advantage of my access changed my view of it.

Day 2 Meditation: Access through God

My "to-do" list last week was perceived as others wanting to stress me out. But having been admitted into this grace God provides, the same "to-do" list is a celebrated revelation of how strong the Lord has made me. So instead of complaining and feeling tired before having expended any energy, I will set my mind to simply "run this race with patience."

This is the spiritual conviction with which I start a new day—blessed to accept the access I have into a grace God provides and to explain my presence there by simply saying I am justified by the plan God imagined before the foundations of the world. That plan is being fulfilled by the sacrificial death of Jesus, who with His resurrection provided me access to live on the other side of my guilt for transgressing His law. I live free to steward my life in pursuit of God's perfect will for me.

Theologian Charles Hodge says, "Access is not mere liberty of approach; it is 'introduction.' Christ did not die simply to open the way of access to God, but actually to introduce us into his presence and favor."

Today, don't let anything make you be like a person locked out of your own house. I do not care what greets you this week. You must walk through your week's journey as you should: like a disciple having been granted access. You will carry no negative emotion longer than your capacity to turn it over to the Lord. You will allow no one space where you have been granted access who does not value this space as sacred and necessary for your life. You will arrest your thoughts and make them surrender to the spiritual space where you have been admitted into this grace. Your thoughts have to dress appropriately, respond obediently, and be guided by the agenda set by the One who extends such powerful grace to me.

I am in my second year of an Allegheny County Appointment to the Pittsburgh Airport Authority Board. Quite often I have to go out to the airport for meetings. The meetings are held in a restricted place that is only accessible with a pictured name badge that grants me entrance. Now, I am also out there often to fly to preaching destinations and have to go plane-side by showing my license and ticket—neither of which can get me into my meetings. But my badge can get me plane-side. When I hang that badge around my neck, I have access to areas that are not accessible without it.

Today, your access is not granted based on your workload, your relational pressures, or your financial challenges. Your access to joy, peace, and productivity is because your heart is full of the presence of Christ. You wear that badge today-flash it when standing in front of restricted spaces, walk into spaces, and engaging conversations that are only possible because God's grace has given you that access.

> **Let us then approach God's throne of grace with confidence, so that we may receive mercy and find grace to help us in our time of need. (Hebrews 4:16).**

QUESTIONS FOR THOUGHT

1. In your own words, what does the grace of God give you access to?

2. Does the thought of this access infuse your energy, lift your spirit, or ignite your drive?

3. Does the time of difficulty you are going through change your access to God's grace?

LET US PRAY

Lord, we affirm and celebrate the access You give us to walk in graced spaces in creation, having been granted access by the work of Christ, who was and is Your "always plan" for our lives. Thank You that You imagined our justification long before even our fall. We stand ready to take on this day acknowledging that we have complete and undeniable access to You given to us not by our perfection but by Your grace.

Give us peace and empower us to represent You with strength and humility. Give us what we need to support each other and make Your voice so dominant in our lives that everything else appears a distraction. Press Your will in our lives and amplify Your Word. Release the Spirit to transform our minds in even deeper ways.

We look not at the things which are seen, but at the things which are unseen: for the things which are seen are temporal, but the things which are not seen are eternal. We want to fix our eyes on the things which are not seen. Lord, open our eyes, still our hands, and steady our feet. We ask it in Jesus' name. Amen.

DAY 3 MEDITATION

THE NEED FOR A SPIRIT BASED ATTITUDE

A.W. Pink said, "Prayer is not so much an act as it is an attitude—an attitude of dependency, dependency upon God."

John Maxwell says, "One's attitude is an inner feeling expressed by behavior!"

Here are some small images describing attitude:

- A chaplain told a young soldier who was lying on a cot, "Son, you lost your right arm in this war." The young soldier said, "No, I kept my left arm in this war."

- A woman asked her Christian neighbor after a car accident, "Aren't you mad at God for this car accident?" The Christian said, "No, I thank God for my life and that I have a car."

- A friend told his coworker, "It's not fair that you didn't get that promotion." The coworker said, "It's not fair that millions of people don't have jobs."

Attitude makes a big difference.

When Paul writes to the church in Philippi, he is driven by a compulsion to teach them how to live with each other in ways that reflect the presence of Christ. Now, remember that the overall theme of the entire epistle of Philippians is to live encouraged because of the presence of Christ at work in the life of a believer. Philippians is written to people who are experiencing severe persecution. Chapter 2 is the encouragement to live despite times of struggle by making one of your offerings to the Lord a right attitude. By attitude, Paul means to have the right "judgments" about your life, circumstances, and human encounters. Remember, John Maxwell's insight that attitude is reflected in behavior.

Paul then teaches what the goal is when it comes to how God expects you to steward your attitude—and it is a lofty goal, to say the least. Here it is: "Have this same attitude in yourselves which was in Christ Jesus [look to Him as your example in selfless humility]". (Philippians 2:5 AMP).

Now let me expand that just a little by showing it in the New International Version, adding verses 6 through 8:

> **In your relationships with one another, have the same mindset as Christ Jesus: Who, being in very nature God, did not consider equality with God something to be used to his own advantage; rather, he made himself nothing by taking the very nature of a servant, being made in human likeness. And being found in appearance as a man, he humbled himself by becoming obedient to death—even death on a cross!**

Jesus' attitude, or inner feeling, was as a servant even though He is God—and that attitude was reflected in His behavior: Jesus humbled Himself and saw the Cross as His response to obeying God's will for human redemption.

How much work needs to be done in that area of your attitude? I have lived long enough to have seen far too many extremely gifted people shackled by debilitating, self-defeating, overinflated, or toxic attitudes. I have often felt so burdened for people that I love dearly who would be so much more advantaged in life if they would make the sacrifice not of effort nor intellect—but of "Spirit-surrendered attitude."

When I think of attitude, I am not suggesting that it should always be what is comfortable for everybody other than yourself or what is not true and authentic to your core personality. There is no greater bondage to me than to be living with an adjusted attitude that makes you inauthentic. What I do, however, want to teach is that the right attitude is a spiritual surrender to the shaping of one's inner feelings, imitating the way Jesus offered His attitude to His Father. Jesus harnessed His inner feelings when on the Cross and suppressed His eternal strength so that He could die a human death. There is no greater example of the control you can have over your attitude than Jesus on the Cross.

This means, when our behavior does not reflect that ethic with which Jesus lived, we have no one to blame but ourselves. No circumstance should make you display an attitude that would make others doubt your spiritual anchoring. There should not be a person alive that should make you agitate the placid waters of your attitude. This to me was the tension between Dr. King and Minister Malcolm. It was not about the "endgame" because of both wanted freedom for oppressed African Americans. Both wanted justice for oppressed people and the right to participate as equal citizens under the law. The endgame was the same for both Dr. King and Minister Malcolm. However, the attitude that gave thrust to that was different. Minister Malcolm's attitude was unapologetically fueled by his anger towards the arrogance and violence of hate-filled white people, whereas Dr. King's attitude was fueled by trying to surrender to an inner feeling of love and compassion toward those same hate-filled white people. Dr. King even confessed at portions of the Movement to how hard that was. My point is that people make them adversaries. It is an argument that I do not believe is productive. Both men died trying to free oppressed people with differing attitudes.

Jesus wants your behavior to be matched with a surrendered attitude. Don't just do the work He is assigning without also offering Him a right attitude as well. Don't just speak when spoken to and respond when requested to but reflect in your behavior that your inner feeling values another person and their good matters to you. You can go many places with a good brain, but that good brain can take you even further still when it is matched by a great attitude. As I consider relationships of deep meaning to me at this stage of my life, attitude is one of the most vital components that sift how far I step into another's space or allow them to do the same in mine.

Harry Emerson Fosdick once told how as a child he was sent by his mother to pick a quart of raspberries. Reluctantly he dragged himself to the berry patch. His afternoon was ruined for sure. Then a thought hit him. He would surprise his mother and pick two quarts of raspberries instead of one. Rather than drudgery, his work now became a challenge. He enjoyed picking those raspberries so much that fifty years later that incident was still fresh in his mind. The job had not changed. His attitude had, demonstrating that an attitude is everything.

J. A. Hadfield gives a striking illustration of this fact in his booklet *The Psychology of Power:* "I asked three people to submit themselves to test the effect of mental suggestion on their strength, which was measured by gripping a dynamometer." They were to grip the dynamometer with all their strength under three different sets of conditions. First, he tested them under normal conditions. The average grip was 101 pounds. Then he tested them after he had hypnotized them and told them that they were weak. Their average grip this time was only 29 pounds. In the third test, Dr. Hadfield told them under hypnosis that they were strong. The average grip jumped to 142 pounds.

My friend, you do not need hypnosis to live convicted about your strengths in an attempt to squeeze the most out of your life. We only need to surrender to the mind of Christ at work in us. "I can do all things through Christ who strengthens me." Now squeeze that truth and live your best life.

QUESTIONS FOR THOUGHT

1. How would you say your attitude has been in the different stages of your current ordeal?

2. How has that attitude shaped your behavior?

3. Do you tend to see yourself as weak, strong, or somewhere in between?

LET US PRAY

Lord, today we make an offering to You of our attitudes! We lay our inner feelings on the altar and ask You to shape us until our behavior reflects the power of Your presence in us. Thank You that You love us enough to want the best for us, and because You do, You have given us the capacity to manipulate our inner feelings and to use them for Your glory and our good.

We, therefore, make the spiritual decision to not be controlled by our circumstances, our relational tensions, or our altered lives while walking through this season. Instead, we cast our glance and press towards the mark of the high calling upon our lives that is exampled in and through the life of Jesus.

Do an amazing work of transformation in our attitudes. No matter how deep You need to dig, and how much You need to excavate, or what You need to pull up, or what You intend to plant, we want to reflect in our behavior attitudes that demonstrate how firmly You are seated on the throne of our inner lives. We pray these things in Jesus' name. Amen.

DAY 4 MEDITATION

OVERCOMING BAD THOUGHTS

Jesus always had a larger group than the twelve men who spent so much time with Him, whose stories we are given, and upon whom the foundation of our institutionalized religion is built. When Jesus knew that the time for crucifixion was closely approaching, we see how wide that net of faithful discipleship was spreading. In Luke 10, Jesus chooses from that larger pool of disciples—consisting of seventy or seventy-two depending on the version-and sends them into the city and closely surrounding villages to share the gospel of salvation and to announce that the kingdom of God had come near to human experience.

When the seventy go out, the mission was successful in its impact on the spread of the gospel. The mission motivated those seventy individuals as they reported with joy that not only were people receptive to the message of the kingdom but even demons were subjected to the name of Jesus. Jesus sensed that He needed to inform them that it would not be an easy mission field moving forward. The seventy would experience opposition the likes of which they had not experienced yet. Jesus knows the power Satan intends to unleash in the earth against their ministries. So rather than allow them to shape their future ministries around the emotional high of easy success, He teaches them that it is not the success that fuels them—it is the spiritual authority that has been given to them by God. Luke 10:17-19 reads:

> **Then the seventy returned with joy, saying, "Lord, even the demons are subject to us in Your name."**
>
> **And He said to them, "I saw Satan fall like lightning from Heaven. Behold, I give you the authority to trample on serpents and scorpions, and over all the power of the enemy, and nothing shall by any means hurt you." (NKJV).**

Do you know what Jesus is teaching them? When the expected is met with opposition, the altered life invades the consistent life that has defined one's history, plans are canceled by things that are out of your control, relationship investments have necessitated more withdrawals than deposits, and the sheer fatigue of it all hits you—then you need more than celebratory victories whether they come easy, as they did for this seventy, or otherwise. Jesus teaches that you need spiritual and mental tenacity. What feeds your spiritual and mental tenacity is the reminder that you are not winning because it is an easy win; you are winning in your life every day because of mental tenacity.

Many people can handle the responsibilities that come with being who they are, but the thin line that separates getting things done from leaving things undone is an issue of tenacity. Some do not possess the mental toughness to work when they do not feel like it, to nurture what does not nurture back, or to give one hundred percent when only fifty percent is necessary, or to make negative thoughts obey them and vacate their mind.

The ability to get things done consistently is not only about passion and excitement; it is about tenacity. I read Luke chapter 10 as a manifesto on mental toughness. I do not think people are necessarily more or less gifted; I think God entrusts them with the fullness of His presence and whatever gifts are associated with that are available for maximum usage at all times based upon the faith they grow to release those gifts. I do, however, think that gifts are manifested differently in the lives of people based upon how a person surrenders to understand their gift and then determines to use their gift and keep that gift sharpened for kingdom purposes. That requires a mental toughness that is wed to spiritual maturity if we follow the image given to us by Luke: to keep following the message when the mission field is not easy and the enemies are not accommodating.

Jesus says that the mental toughness you possess is of such a nature that you can tread on serpents and scorpions, and exercise authority over the power of Satan-nothing will harm you. That is the mental toughness you possess right now. You have that capacity in you at this moment.

It does not mean to walk on a scorpion, a serpent, or to stand opposite Satan. It means to face their environmental or experiential parallels in *your* life. Jesus is suggesting that you have because of Him the mental toughness to not let the serpent engage your life, and make you doubt the presence and power of your God-as Adam and Eve did. You ought to live every day knowing that while you will have to deal with that mental battle, you go into it with the capacity to crush its head before it bruises your heel. That is how mentally tough you are. You can engage every day beating the enemy's attempt to ruin, stress, or conflict it. You can beat the enemy to it. Make choices that will bring joy, peace, and focus to the day.

You can shape how the conversation is going to go, so you do not have to wait to "see how things go." You can decide that despite the load, you will carry it like it is not heavy! Jesus is not trying to steal your celebration. When things go as easy for you as they did for the seventy, then you ought to celebrate and enjoy the absence of struggle and hard engagement. But when it is not easy, then you have the mental toughness to exercise your spiritual authority and get it done anyway—even if by having to fight for it. You are not just spiritually connected but you are mentally tough. How tough? Serpent-head-crushing, scorpion-foot-stomping tough! How tough? Satan-can't-do-me-harm tough.

How do you accept and appropriate this authority? By walking in the grace of it enough to exercise it. Here is the key: Me telling you that you are mentally tough is not enough. Exposing it to you in Scripture is not enough.

Day 4 Meditation: Overcoming Bad Thoughts

You have to stand in the stressful and uncomfortable places in your life and decide to take the chance and exercise your spiritual authority. You have to feel the anxiety rising in your life, the negativity squeezing in, the anger swelling up, the feeling sorry for yourself starting to circle your thoughts, the feeling of defeat teasing and taunting. When you feel these things, only you can decide to exercise your authority and let your mental toughness engage these thoughts in a war for what kind of day you are going to have. So the question is not "Did you receive this word for your life?" The question is "Are you going to exercise the authority that was revealed from it?"

I love the quote that says, "Mental toughness is when you can find fuel in an empty tank."

A schoolteacher injured his back and had to wear a plaster cast around the upper part of his body. It fit under his shirt and was not noticeable. On the first day of the term, still with the cast under his shirt, the schoolteacher found himself assigned to the toughest students in school. Walking confidently into the rowdy classroom, he opened the window as wide as possible and then busied himself with desk work. When a strong breeze made his tie flap, he took the desk stapler and stapled the tie to his chest.

He had no trouble with discipline that term.

I am not suggesting you wake up tomorrow and try that, but I want you to know how tough you are and what kind of spiritual cast you wear under your clothing.

Finally, be strong in the Lord and in his mighty power. Put on the full armor of God, so that you can take your stand against the devil's schemes. For our struggle is not against flesh and blood, but against the rulers, against the authorities, against the powers of this dark world and against the spiritual forces of evil in the Heavenly realms. Therefore put on the full armor of God, so that when the day of evil comes, you may be able to stand your ground, and after you have done everything, to stand. Stand firm then, with the belt of truth buckled around your waist, with the breastplate of righteousness in place, and with your feet fitted with the readiness that comes from the gospel of peace. In addition to all this, take up the shield of faith, with which you can extinguish all the flaming arrows of the evil one. Take the helmet of salvation and the sword of the Spirit, which is the word of God.

And pray in the Spirit on all occasions with all kinds of prayers and requests. With this in mind, be alert and always keep on praying for all the Lord's people. (Ephesians 6:10-18).

QUESTIONS FOR THOUGHT

1. What are some of the easier victories you have had that bolster your confidence and taught you that, with the Lord's help, you can handle the difficult battles?

2. Does every day feel like a mental and spiritual uphill climb?

3. Have you yet decided to exert tenacity, no matter how hard it gets?

LET US PRAY

Lord, today we do not just pray to be filled with the Spirit and to walk by faith. We do not just ask You to bless us and use us, to protect us and guard us. We pray also for You to make us mentally strong! Help us to not just search for You in the easy engagements of our lives, but to know You have given us authority when what is necessary is to fight to advance Your purposes and to protect Your gifting in us and to proclaim Your goodness during really tough times.

Help us to accept how mentally tough we are, that it may construct a powerful perspective in our lives, removing the sting of the constant fight and struggle, taking the dread out of the constant need to show up and perform at high levels, taking the stress out of being pulled on for everything by everybody. Continue to allow the Spirit to bring this word to our remembrance; that You have given us authority—mental toughness—to protect our lives even against the mental assaults Satan drops on us. We are encouraged today not because demons were subject to Your name all day today, but we rejoice because we spent all day "seated and clothed in our right minds." Thank You for making us so tough. We love You for it. We pray this in Jesus' name. Amen.

DAY 5 MEDITATION

DEFINING YOUR WIN

The success of the civil rights movement was aided by the fact that there was a clear picture of what constituted progress and what a "win" looked like. Voting rights, housing, and education were the targets. Everybody nationally gathered around those pillars.

Similarly, it was clear for Jesus what the win was. It was to declare the arrival of the kingdom of God on Earth. It was to reveal God's intentional favor on the oppressed. The empty tomb was the sign of the win.

In John 12:27-32, Jesus said:

> **Now my soul is troubled, and what shall I say? "Father, save me from this hour"? No, it was for this very reason I came to this hour. Father, glorify your name!**

Then a voice came from heaven, "I have glorified it, and will glorify it again." The crowd that was there and heard it said it had thundered; others said an angel had spoken to him.

Jesus said, "This voice was for your benefit, not mine. Now is the time for judgment on this world; now the prince of this world will be driven out. And I, when I am lifted up from the earth, will draw all people to myself."

I ask you; What does a "win" in your life look like? What is the Red Sea opening for you? What will be the sign that you are standing one step from Canaan? What is the win that signals the need to shift attention and to change strategy or to lift the reach that Jesus so clearly has graced us with? No miracle, message, or meandering around defined the win for Jesus. The win for Him was this: "If I am lifted from the earth, I will draw all humanity to me." Of course, we know that meant crucifixion, resurrection, and ascension, all of which secured our human redemption.

I am pushing you today to change your musings. I do not want you to spend your whole life defining, accepting, and living despite your losses. You are in a relationship with Christ who wants to help you define your wins. What is a win for you? Is it to provide an uncluttered runway for your child or children to give them a chance to lift and launch without the weight that kept you grounded for so long? Is it to fight systems of oppression, or to conquer mental illness in your life? I would hope for you that a win is the same as it is for me: to live the rest of your life with the "director's cut" of the movie called "You."

If you could not get an audience with God to talk about your losses anymore for the rest of your life and only had one chance meeting with God to ask Him for the one thing that would define a win for you in life, then what would you talk to the Lord about? That is the revelation of your calling. The explanation for the gifts that have been entrusted to you, the justification for your placement in life, the definition of your spacing in life. It will explain your relationships, and their interesting twists and encounters.

I want you to think about this because you need to know what a win is for you. If you eliminated the stressors in your life, controlled every physical challenge, had a less stressful schedule, were surrounded by people who give you a lift in life, could find the mental strength to accept the way you are uniquely framed and formed, could eulogize your regrets and praise God for His grace, then would you declare that the big win in your life?

I cannot define that for you. It is different for every one of us. But I know this: you will only attract to your life what you discern is the reason God has made you a living sacrifice. It is what Dr. King meant when he suggested that you do not know what you are alive for until you are convicted of what you will die for.

I am critiquing traditional attempts to always enter through the back door of pain, struggle, fatigue, and stress. Let's enter through the front door of vision. Define the endgame. What's the win? Build your future from there.

Dr. Liz Theoharis, along with Dr. William Barber, gives leadership to the National Poor People's Campaign. Theoharis said:

> **The New Testament...portrays the survival struggles of the marginalized, the solidarity and mutuality among different communities, and the critique of a social, political, and economic system that oppresses the vast majority of people.... Jesus's teachings and actions around poverty, wealth, and power create a picture of**

him as a leader of a social, political, economic, and spiritual movement calling for a world without poverty, want, or oppression...what he named the Kingdom or Empire of God.

Do you hear how clear the win is for Jesus? I want you to identify what a win is for you! By faith don't settle for anything less than a win!

QUESTIONS FOR THOUGHT

1. What is the win, the endgame, for your life?

2. What do you think God's endgame is for your current struggle?

3. How can you stay focused on your resolve to reach the goal?

LET US PRAY

Lord, I pray that You help us to make the vision for our lives so plain that it creates a conviction about who we are and why we live the way we do. Help us to resist being pulled in so many directions, led by our passion until we miss where You have gifted and planted us to represent Your kingdom.

Still, our minds today and calm our raging tensions. Settle our anxieties and give us peace that surpasses all human understanding so that we can define what ultimately makes Your heart happy about our lives. You made winning possible for us in Your death and resurrection. We want to win and we know that means seeking first Your kingdom and its righteousness. Today we recommit ourselves to that. Grant us a peaceful and productive day in You. We love You today and always. In Jesus' name, we pray. Amen.

DAY 6 MEDITATION

HOLDING YOUR THOUGHTS CAPTIVE

I start our time together today with a quote by first-century Latin writer Syrus, who said, "He conquers twice who conquers himself."

Muse on those words for a moment. We know one of the assumptions Syrus raises in that quote is that we are always fighting on two fronts in life. We have external battles we face each day and in addition to that there is an internal front. We attempt to give direction and leadership to the frantic motion of our thoughts swirling about so many things that it seems difficult to catch our breath. You forget to do what positively nurtures your spirit. You forget that you are also your first ministry offering to God along with what you do for others. Self-care and sacrificing for others are both of the highest priorities.

My conviction is not only to help you navigate these times by following a spiritual compass but to also process your thinking theologically. That is, seeking to understand your faith as you wrestle with all of the struggles, tensions, and relationships you navigate each day, or as Syrus so wisely says "to win the battle twice".

Paul understood this when writing to a culture not too dissimilar from ours. Corinth was the socially diverse seaport providing a fun stop on the way to places to handle merchant exchange. In this bustling seaport city, Paul tried to teach followers of Christ how to live out their faith in Jesus. Paul faced unbelievable opposition and criticism from a minority of highly vocal opponents to his ministry who thought Paul was bold in his letters but seemed to back down in person from confrontation. They wanted to agitate Paul in hopes of drawing him into a battle that would tempt him to act opposite of the Christ he was trying to follow.

Paul almost said to them what we often imply to each other at times. Paul suggested that they not think that they cannot fight according to the flesh. That is code for "I could battle that way if I wanted to." But Paul quickly admits that he has transcended that flesh-dominating way of processing human disagreement and has instead yielded to following the example of his Christ who surrendered the physical way by obediently dying on the cross and exampled the spiritual way of displaying conquering love. Then Paul revealed how he won battles twice every time he engaged them: "We demolish arguments and every pretension that sets itself up against the knowledge of God, and we take captive every thought to make it obedient to Christ" (II Corinthians 10:5).

How does Paul win the battles in his life? Battles that are fought both in his external world with this minority sect of agitators that so strongly oppose him, and in his internal thoughts that are always being tempted to engage these opponents in his flesh? How does Paul fight his perceptions when he is called to lead where he does not want to and called to love who he does not want to, and called to be an encourager when he wants to rest in surrendered cynicism?

Paul says that you fight it by accepting that it is your fight to engage. It starts with deciding which of your thoughts need to be held captive and which thoughts you let exist unrestrained. We can tell a lot about your direction and assumptions regarding life by which thoughts you have decided must be held *captive.* Interestingly, Paul used the word captive. Paul does not say that you should not think about something counterproductive and maybe even destructive. Paul says do not just give it a long leash, but believe that you must bring it into captivity.

This word *captive* means to make it a prisoner. Captive paints the image of a strategy for war, where you are not chasing the enemy away, but you are trying to ensnare the enemy—trying to trap your thoughts and lock them under guard.

You have to put some thoughts under guard, locked away so they are not wandering around the field where you are dreaming—away from the affirming thoughts you spent all day planting. You cannot let certain perceptions walk around free in your thoughts, unmonitored and unrestrained, until they have you believing false things.

I have done that. I have allowed thoughts to have too much space, voice, and influence until I made the perception my truth. Then, when I heard the real truth, it did not matter because the perception had become my truth.

If you feed a perception enough, then it will become your truth. Paul says that when you walk by faith in the Lord Jesus Christ, then the Holy Spirit gives you the power to take your thoughts captive. How do you guard them? You place the obedience of Christ as a guard.

This simply means I must sift my thoughts through a Christlike mindset at all times. Not my emotions, my reasoning, and my reflex response, unless I have nurtured a reflex response that bends towards a Christlike way of looking at things first. What makes you a Christian is knowing what thoughts to take captive, and once taking them captive, setting those thoughts before Christ and then making the choice that reflects obedience to Him.

Be bold about owning which thoughts you are going to take captive today.

- I am going to take captive every thought that deflates my faith potential.

- I am going to take captive every thought that makes me see people out of my disappointment for how people can act and how some have acted towards me.

- I am going to take captive every thought that shows people a part of me that is not Christlike.

- I am going to take captive every thought that invites me to a decision that tries to push the Lord out of having direct influence over that decision.

- I am going to take captive every thought that makes me feel like I am not controlling the movement and influence of my thoughts.

These are but a few ways to take your thoughts captive. You can add more to ensure that today is a day of control for you. Either take every thought captive and make it obedient or if a thought gets away and starts running wild, then hold yourself captive to protect the damage that wild thought may create. Either way, it is that battle that I want you to win. Jesus will help you win the battle in the areas where He directly intervenes. However, in the areas where He allows your thoughts to launch an attack, then the decision is yours as to what you do with your thoughts.

Read Paul's words in *The Message* version:

> **The world is unprincipled. It's dog-eat-dog out there! The world doesn't fight fair. But we don't live or fight our battles that way—never have and never will. The tools of our trade aren't for marketing or manipulation, but they are**

for demolishing that entire massively corrupt culture. We use our powerful God tools for smashing warped philosophies, tearing down barriers erected against the truth of God, fitting every loose thought and emotion, and impulse into the structure of life shaped by Christ. Our tools are ready at hand for clearing the ground of every obstruction and building lives of obedience into maturity. (II Corinthians 10:3-6).

QUESTIONS FOR THOUGHT

1. Are you fighting a battle on two fronts in your current hardship? Describe your internal and external struggle.

2. Which thoughts do you repeatedly have to bring into captivity?

3. What will eventually happen to thoughts that are not held captive?

LET US PRAY

Lord, thank You for reminding us that we can control the management and stewardship of our thoughts. We covenant with You to take our thoughts captive when they attempt to go contrary to Your will and way. For making us strong in the spirit, we say thank You. Even now help us to make decisions that bring resistance to perceptions and thoughts that are so counterproductive in and for our lives.

We hear You say to us that we are strong in You and the power of Your might. That You have given us authority and entrusted us with talents and endowed our lives with gifts and made us witnesses to Your presence in the Earth. Because these are the things we are thinking of right now, we will not let anything make us doubt Your goodness and grace or Your plan and will for our lives.

You are mighty in us to deliver and because of this, we affirm that it is going to be a great day walking with You and discovering the new ways You will display Your grace and dispense Your presence and power. We are more than ready! We pray in Jesus' name. Amen.

DAY 7 MEDITATION

JOURNALING YOUR JOURNEY

Today, spend time in prayer and reflection on what you have digested in this week's meditations. Record your thoughts, emotions, insights, and prayers on the following pages. "Journaling your journey" through this difficult time in your life not only serves to help you process your experience at the moment but will be something you can look back on in the future as evidence of how God has worked in your life.

_____

_____

_____

_____

Day 7 Meditation: Journaling Your Journey

_____

_____

_____

_____

_____

_____

_____

_____

_____

_____

_____

_____

_____

_____

_____

_____

_____

_____

_____

_____

_____

_____

_____

Day 7 Meditation: Journaling Your Journey

_____

_____

_____

_____

_____

_____

_____

_____

_____

_____

_____

DAY 8 MEDITATION

MOVING WITH COMPASSION

Mark chapter 1 will have you short of breath if you try to run at the pace of Jesus. Straight out of baptism waters and led by the Spirit into the wilderness, Jesus had an intense inner battle with Satan about the interpretation of Scripture, the meaning of ministry, and the motives of the human heart.

When Jesus returned from that battle in the wilderness, He was told immediately that John had been arrested. Jesus went straight to Galilee and preached. But, what Jesus preached is defiantly rebellious and sets a tone for what would be the antagonistic relationship He would have with religious leaders. When we hear those words "the kingdom of God is at hand," we breathe a sigh of relief. When His adversaries heard Jesus say that, they knew the culture was about to experience sharp tension. Lines were drawn in the sand; it was equivalent to stating a declaration of war.

No sooner had Jesus finished preaching than He walked along the water's edge calling Andrew and Peter to be disciples. Jesus was adding learners that for three years will make withdrawals of His virtue, demands on His time, a stretching of His patience, and will dig deep entrenchments of meaning in His heart—so much so that He will say to them that He has ceased calling them disciples and will now refer to them as friends. Mark tells us that James and John were added right after. We are only at verse 21 in the first chapter. Jesus walked into the synagogue and is tapped to teach. What was poured out from Jesus was so unique that His authority was discerned by those who hear Him. Whenever that much authority is present, it draws people who are locked in spiritual spaces because of the dominance of evil. Jesus was confronted with a man with an unclean spirit. The authority Jesus possessed was displayed and the man was freed.

When they left the synagogue, it was straight to Peter's house where Jesus was immediately met with the sickness of Peter's mother-in-law and He healed her. By now word had spread of Jesus' presence, His authority over unclean spirits, His teaching, His call of essential workers in town, and by evening there was a steady stream of people bringing the sick and demon-possessed to Him. Mark said the crowd was so thick that it looked like it was the whole town. Jesus healed as many as possible in the time He ministered.

Then we read that early the next morning while it was still dark, Jesus got up, went out, found a secluded place, and settled in for prayer. We know why, don't we? Because in only thirty-five verses, there has been that much activity, spiritual battle, teaching, calling, ministering, and moving about.

It's overwhelming. It is one challenge after another. It is having to show up and be at maximum strength everywhere. It is knowing your mission and not letting demand make you forget the need for self-care. It is knowing your limit and having enough discernment to know when you need to isolate and reconnect with your spiritual reservoir. When Peter finds the Master, Jesus immediately said, "Let's go to the neighboring towns and let's duplicate there what we just did here." We know that for three years this will be the pace. This made the story that followed revelatory, because He goes throughout Galilee preaching in the synagogues, casting out demons, and that was Mark's way of saying that He kept the same pace moving forward that He did in those initial thirty-five verses. Then in verses 40 and 41, we read:

> **And a leper came to Him, begging Him and falling on his knees before Him, saying, "If You are willing, You are able to make me clean." Moved with compassion [for his suffering], Jesus reached out with His hand and touched him, and said to him, "I am willing; be cleansed." (AMP).**

All of this high intensity, high emotion, high confrontation, constant demand, rapid-paced deeply engaged connection with intense human suffering— people pouring and piling sickness and demon-possessed realities at His feet, and every single one expecting what He gave to the one before them: complete restoration and healing. To show up everywhere, all the time, with all of your authority, and do again what you just did. We get a clue of how draining it was because Jesus does not even tell anybody how much it had cost Him; He just snuck out and got in God's presence where He got what He needed.

But Mark tells us how Jesus kept His edge and how He never let the work become an emotionless string of activity. Mark tells us how Jesus stayed personally powerful while being powerfully present everywhere, all the time. It was because He never let the tremendous pull or the monotonous repetition of it all empty Him of *compassion.*

"Moved with compassion." That is so surprising, given the number of healings, including almost a whole town, the non-stop action, the high-energy spiritual battles against unclean spirits, and the blood-rushing adrenalin of watching people grab your teaching, not to mention the proud moment of watching fishermen walk away from what they thought was the thrill of life and knowing that they were about to be introduced to what would make that pale insignificance. Jesus never let any of it rob Him of His compassion.

With all of the demands, pressures, and fatiguing pull that your time of hardship is forcing on you, Jesus teaches that what keeps you able to get up early the next morning, what restores your joy and revives your sense of purpose, is to never lose your compassion for others.

That was the power Mark revealed in this meditation text today. That man with leprosy approached and begged for Jesus to heal him, and despite all that

Jesus had confronted and been confronted by, He was "moved with compassion."

I want you to find your strength there in this season; it will filter your entire experience. It will keep you hopeful and will not let cynicism take you prisoner. Stoking the flames of your compassion will help you to smile about a bright future and to see life beyond the sadness. Don't let whatever your struggles are pushing you to a place where you are no longer led by, or moved, with compassion.

The Holy Spirit lets you feel or be moved in the inward parts; that is what it refers to in the Greek: the seat of your affections. It is to encounter the vilest aspects of people yet be moved to treat them in a way that reflects the want for Jesus to use them in life-altering ways. It is to take care of a sick one and to not let the repetition of the work make you distant, cold, and absent of a caring spirit. It is to be so disappointed in the actions of another and naturally want to respond in ways that would reveal your disappointment, but to instead understand that people are flawed–they have bad days and are often misinformed. It is to know that some are intentionally motivated to irritate and agitate you, but they are still worth compassionate investment.

Jesus gave us a clear example as to how we protect this space in our lives when He got up early in the morning, went out to the solitary place, and prayed there alone.

You protect your capacity to be led by and moved by your compassion, by disciplining your life to get in spaces where God can recalibrate your emotions and remind you of how He wants to love and use you. It is there that mission and meaning are redefined. You are reminded of how important you are to God. I want you to relate to others and interpret your circumstances by being moved with compassion. Engage your conversations, shape your protest, and challenge those around you and your convictions–but be moved with compassion.

There is a Chinese proverb that says, "A bit of fragrance always clings to the hand that gives roses."

Born over 60 years ago in Yugoslavia, she responded to God's call on her life while still a teenager. A missionary's strong challenge to give her life to teaching in India resulted in her appointment to the city of Calcutta. Some months later, she saw a sight which completely revolutionized her life and would ultimately

bring her worldwide fame as *Good Housekeeping* magazine's "Most Admired Woman" selection.

What was the sight? A homeless, dying woman lying in the gutter, being eaten by rats. Compassion compelled her to beg for possession of an abandoned Hindu temple from the government and convert it into a crude makeshift hospital for the dying. A comment of hers became her life's thrust: "If there is a God in Heaven, and a Christ we love, nobody should die alone."

This woman who established colonies for over 10,000 lepers in 28 cities was interviewed by Malcolm Muggeridge from the BBC News. "Mother Teresa, the thing I noticed about you and the hundreds of sisters who now form your team is that you all look so happy. Is that a put-on?"

She replied, "Oh no, not at all. Nothing makes you happier than when you really reach out in mercy to someone who is badly hurt." Service is its own reward. True mercy begets genuine joy.

"Instead of putting others in their place, put yourself in their place." This is what the Lord expects of us because "compassion is the passion with a heart."

QUESTIONS FOR THOUGHT

1. Are there some in your life who seem especially abrasive, abusive, misunderstanding, or unfeeling during this difficult time you are going through?

2. What is standing in the way of you looking on others with compassion today?

3. Is there someone you know who exemplifies compassion? Someone you can try to emulate?

LET US PRAY

Lord, our prayer today is that in these difficult times, help us to never wax cold in our compassion. Give us what we need to bring those with whom we have exchange into our inner beings so that we hear more than words, see more than expressions, and discern more than emotions. Help us pull on the Spirit's presence to make us discern and to live with Your authority that gives us the license to walk in that heavenly sphere above the challenges, crises, and stresses of this world. Help us to extend more than our ear and our assistance, but to extend our hearts as well.

To that end, make us powerful representatives of compassion. Don't let us become weary because of the nonstop difficulties we face. Build-in us the capacity to talk, lead, and love with compassion. We ask it in Jesus' name. Amen.

DAY 9 MEDITATION

THE LOVE OF GOD IN YOUR LIFE

A television documentary of David's life would have to be a multiple-episode project since there are so many details of his life that shaped the gifted psalmist and king. From his anointing to his dreadful mistakes, David's story is one of a man who had to fight so much in life. This is what created the robust content of so many of his songs. David is a man who had to wrestle hard with his internal contradictions. As a result, his songs are deeply transforming for those who sing them. David was as much loved as he was envied; he was hunted as much as he was heralded.

At one portion of his life, David sits as a celebrated king who reflects on all the ways God has been so extraordinarily good to him. David could have given himself to this kind of musing because, the Bible says,

God had given him rest from all of his enemies. Scholars believe that this is following seven years of wars and battles with nations that surrounded Israel. Finally, David sat in his palace and it crossed his mind that the ark of God remained in a tent. The ark of God was believed to be the presence of God. In the ark were the tablets containing the law. David felt unsettled enjoying the palace while the presence of God was in a tent.

David shared his musings with Nathan the prophet. Nathan's response to David was "Whatever you are thinking about doing, do it, because the Lord is with you." But that night God spoke to the prophet and told him to instruct David that God does not want anything built by David to house His presence; for that time He preferred to dwell in a tent. After reminding David of all that He has done for him, God says that David's son will build Him a house instead. Listen to what God says He will do for David's offspring, Solomon.

> **He will be the one to build a temple honoring My name, and I will establish the leadership of his kingdom for all time. I will be to him a father, and he will be to Me a son. When he crosses the line and acts badly, I will teach him with a rod used by**

people for correction and a lash for discipline. (II Samuel 7:13-14 VCE).

Can you imagine hearing this from the prophet as God's message to you about your child? David had to feel "I can't help but praise Him" excitement. One more verse contains the words we all need to carry as a daily affirmation for our own lives because it transcends everything we are going through in times of difficulty. It transcends everything you are feeling, from anxiety to anticipation:

But my love will never be taken away from him, as I took it away from Saul, whom I removed from before you. (II Samuel 7:15 VCE).

It must have excited David to hear that his son Solomon, who would build God a house and sit upon the throne and have the anointing of God upon his life, would never experience the possibility of losing the love of God in his life.

That was God's promise to David. David watched a king lose God's presence and witnessed the human wreck King Saul became as a result of it. It would not have mattered if God had spelled out for David every war that Solomon was going to face and how he would emerge from them. It would not have mattered if God revealed to David how rich Solomon would become, how much land he would occupy, and how much wisdom he would possess. Nothing can compare to this: God's promise to never take His love from him.

I want you to hear that for your own life today because God makes that same promise to you. God promises that no matter what shifts and shakes, threatens, and taunts, no matter what is being spewed and spread, then you will never be without the love of God in your life.

Where is God in all that is going on in your life? God is where God was before you entered this season. God is in the hearts of His people, and nothing will threaten that. The things you are experiencing may shake everything you know, but it cannot shake the fact that we are always living with the love of God.

You cannot think of anything that will erode His love. You cannot make a big enough mistake. You cannot lift enough doubt or express enough fear that would diminish the love God has for you. You cannot raise questions about His motives or actions that will make Him not love you.

Everything in your life that is pressure, threat, fear, doubt, concern, worry, frustration, angst, and whatever else you add to the list—it is penultimate. That means it is second to last. What is last and most significant in your thinking is the love God has for you! As a Christian, every experience in your life is "second last," including the trial you are facing.

This is what feeds hope. When you are convicted that you are never in jeopardy of losing the love of God, then you stare at present reality and give a defiant glance because you are imagining life beyond it. This is what I want to encourage you to do: don't build hope on things that are penultimate but build your hope on the steadfast love of God in your life.

Corrie ten Boom shares her reflection when she says: "Often I have heard people say, 'How good God is! We prayed that it would not rain for our church picnic and look at the lovely weather!' Yes, God is good when He sends good weather. But God was also good when He allowed my sister, Betsie, to starve to death before my eyes in a German concentration camp. I remember one occasion when I was very discouraged there. Everything around us was dark, and there was darkness in my heart. I remember telling Betsie that I thought God had forgotten us. 'No, Corrie,' said Betsie, 'He has not forgotten us. Remember His Word: "For as the heavens are high above the earth, so great is His steadfast love toward those who fear Him."

Corrie concluded, "There is an ocean of God's love available—there is plenty for everyone. May God grant you never to doubt that victorious love, whatever the circumstances."

Psalm 103 says:

> **O my soul, bless God.**
>
> **From head to toe, I'll bless his holy name!**
>
> **O my soul, bless God,**
>
> **don't forget a single blessing!**
>
> **He forgives your sins—every one.**
>
> **He heals your diseases—every one.**
>
> **He redeems you from hell—saves your life!**
>
> **He crowns you with love and mercy—a paradise crown.**
>
> **He wraps you in goodness—beauty eternal.**
>
> **He renews your youth—you're always young in his presence.**

God makes everything come out right;
he puts victims back on their feet.

He showed Moses how he went about his work,
opened up his plans to all Israel.

God is sheer mercy and grace;
not easily angered, he's rich in love.

He doesn't endlessly nag and scold,
nor hold grudges forever.

He doesn't treat us as our sins deserve,
nor pay us back in full for our wrongs.

As high as Heaven is over the Earth,
so strong is his love to those who fear him. (MSG).

Everything about our lives and surrounding our lives is second last to this: you will always have the love of God in your life. His love was strong enough to break Satan's hold on your life, so you know it is strong enough to get you through this time you are living in.

QUESTIONS FOR THOUGHT

1. **How do you know that God will never take His love away from you?**

2. **What do you feel when you consider that you can depend on God's love?**

3. **What are some of the penultimate things that try to vie for your attention and concern?**

LET US PRAY

Lord, we thank You today for Your steadfast love and we believe that as high as the heavens are from the earth, that is how great Your love is for us. Teach us to live with this affirmation and to let it speak first in response to our fears and frustrations. Today, I pray that Your love is easily discerned and powerfully demonstrated. May it infuse our faith and expand our hope so that rather than live in this tense time only reacting to things as they unfold, we can accept Your invitation to imagine the season beyond this hardship and personal challenge.

We stand strengthened by Your love, we imagine a life full of joy, happiness, growth, and meaningful relationships. Bless us to live always with this reminder first and foremost in our thinking. You have promised that Your love can never be taken away from us and we love You for it. In Jesus' name, we pray. Amen.

DAY 10 MEDITATION

GOD IS FIGHTING FOR YOU

In Moab, forty days before Israel is to first enter the land of Canaan, at 120 years of age, Moses knows he will soon make his life's transition into eternity. Moses took the opportunity to call together these nomadic people, who are in the infancy stage of becoming a nation called to live as the chosen people of God. The Israelites were chosen to live in covenant with God and Moses recounted for them the past forty years. While talking about God's activity in the lives of these people over forty years, Moses used the time to let that theological reflection frame Israel's ethical underpinnings. Theology always informs ethics. How we think about God informs not only what we know about God but how we live out that understanding and how we relate to other people.

Moses wanted this exercise to create a deep hunger in Israel to live in obedience to God. Israelites were standing on the border of promise with a future as pregnant with possibility as they can imagine. The Israelites had been fortunate to have been chosen by God, who wanted to live in covenant with them. All that God required was a steadfast commitment to the covenant relationship they shared with Him, lived out in devoted adherence to God's laws for a community built on what Gregory Boyle, who leads Homeboy Industries in Los Angeles, describes when he says, "It would seem that quite possibly, the ultimate measure of health in any community might well reside in our ability to stand in awe at what folks have to carry rather than in judgment at how they carry it!"

Moses reflected over forty years of God inviting Israel to live in that kind of community. For Moses, there were essentially three reasons to reflect, rehearse, and then renew the covenant they have with God: 1) God's history of goodness to His people, 2) the goodness of God's laws, and 3) God's unconditional promises of blessings for the future. While Moses was doing all of this reflecting, rehearsing, and calling for renewal, he keeps hitting a dominant subtheme. You hear it in Deuteronomy 3:22: "Do not be afraid of them; the Lord your God himself will fight for you."

I woke up at 5:34 this morning and was forced by the Spirit out of bed. When I grabbed my laptop and opened the Scriptures, it fell open as if by divine design to Deuteronomy 3:22. As clear as I am talking to you today, I felt like the Spirit was rushing me and pushing me: "Come on, start shaping and configuring this revelation. Hurry up and yawn and stretch. No, you can't use the bathroom yet. Don't you ever forget that I am fighting for you."

Moses must have believed this at his core because he knew the people were about to cross over to the land he knew was forbidden from stepping into. While Moses was commissioning Joshua about his role in keeping Israel committed to the covenant they shared with God—with so much to say about so many things. Moses said to them, "Here is what you can be assured of: God will fight for you!"

I hope you feel that in your soul while you are processing, progressing, pushing, and producing. While you are scratching and clawing and showing up in this world the best you know-how. While you are getting it done the best way you can and standing up every day knowing how many times you are being knocked down. While you are trying to figure it out and wishing others would just get it and understand you and treat you accordingly. While you wish it could be more days without the uphill climb and fewer days with the attacks and pressures, let me tell you this: the Lord is fighting for you.

God knows how much you want to enjoy Canaan, eat its fruit, and live free of the pressures, pains, and prisons of your current circumstances. He wants you to fight knowing He is fighting for you. Did you catch that? He's fighting for you does not take the fight away from you, but it sure changes how you fight. You fight with greater resolve, deeper conviction, and with a hope cast towards the future because God is also fighting for you. Just knowing you have His presence, His support, and His understanding of what you are fighting against should be awe-inspiring and spirit-moving. I always am ready to go at it when I know God is fighting for me.

I am in my fifties. I have had so many blessed experiences in life that it seems unreal. But can I tell you that I do not go too many days without seeing again that day some friends and I were out back shooting the ball on a makeshift basketball goal. Some older young adults started hurling rocks down on us from a perched position above, on the alley side of the railroad tracks. I do not know if we were mouthing loudly in response at them, though we were significantly younger. It aroused the attention of all three of our fathers. I will never forget my dad, Mr. Woods, and Mr. White all coming out back and running up that hill and across those tracks. Whatever transpired on the other side, we never were made aware of but several minutes later it was apparent that they had fought for us.

That story is matched by another that is always connected to me. I saw Rodney Bulls' dad sitting on his porch with ice on his right hand when I got home from school one day. I did not know until later that our house had been broken into. Unfortunately for the thief, it was on the wrong day when the neighbor to our left, Mr. Bulls, was off of work. He saw a man carrying my father's 8-track stereo system out the back door. By the time my father had gotten home, our system was back in the house and the door was being guarded by Mr. Bulls, who fought for our family.

I paint these pictures for you because I want you to know that while you are trying to simply make it through this season the best you know-how with the help of the Lord, God sees what is being thrown at you and He is chasing whatever constitutes enemy intent in your life.

Whatever is breaking in on your life, be it emotional or otherwise, be encouraged and infused with renewed hope and stronger faith, because the Lord is fighting for you.

- What, then, shall we say in response to these things? If God is for us, then who can be against us? (Romans 8:31).

- "For the Lord your God is the one who goes with you to fight for you against your enemies to give you victory." (Deuteronomy 20:4).

- "Have I not commanded you? Be strong and courageous. Do not be afraid; do not be discouraged, for the Lord your God will be with you wherever you go." (Joshua 1:9).

- "You are from God, little children, and have overcome them; because greater is He who is in you than he who is in the world." (1 John 4:4).

QUESTIONS FOR THOUGHT

1. Can you recall an instance in your past when someone fought for you?

2. Is it hard to believe that God is fighting for you at this moment when circumstances seem otherwise?

3. In what ways can you stand in defense of others and fight for them?

LET US PRAY

Lord, thank You for giving us a chance to breathe amidst all the things that stand in opposition to us. Our eyes are not dim, and our strength has not been abated. We feel an incredible sense of renewed energy because You are fighting for us. Our joy is restored as we sit with Moses instructing Joshua and giving final teaching points on our need to remember You, to obey You, and to trust You—that You are so strong and mighty. You are at work every day in us to perform Your good pleasure in our lives.

Day 10 Meditation: God is Fighting for You

Today, our fight is renewed. We are more than ready to engage another day, another season, another ministry assignment because we know we have a fight in us with You fighting for us. Thank You, for being our might. It sure helps to feed our faith to know that the battles are not ours but Yours. It is in Jesus' name we pray. Amen.

DAY 11 MEDITATION

LISTENING TO GOD OR YELLING AT GOD?

We have the Book of Numbers because it describes God's presence and activity in the lives of Israel in that space between being delivered from Egypt and settling in Canaan. These were hard years because God was working to get them ready for the land of promise, but they have so much rebellion and obstinance in them that it took forty years and the death of a generation to prepare them. It is why the Book of Numbers has also been referred to as the Book of Murmurings—because these rebellious people spent an inordinate amount of time complaining about everything from the difficulty of the journey to the style of leadership provided to them by Moses. Moses got so frustrated with them during this gap between deliverance and possession that he exposed fatal flaws in his character by letting his anger make him loosen his obedience. This cost him the chance to step into the land he was leading Israel towards.

So that Israel had a symbol of God's presence and active voice in their lives, Moses was led to build what was called the "Tent of Meeting". It was believed by Israel to be the place where Moses would meet with God and receive instruction, listen to God's voice, and interpret revelation in ways that would be easy to communicate to the people. This tabernacle was forty-five feet long and fifteen feet wide, with a courtyard in front of it. The forecourt contained a lampstand, incense altar, and a table with twelve loaves of bread representing the twelve tribes of Israel. The inner court housed the ark of the covenant, which contained the tablets on which the Ten Commandments were written. The Israelites took the Tent of Meeting with them as they traveled through the wilderness from Mount Sinai to Canaan.

I only provide this brief description because Israel knew that when Moses entered the Tent of Meeting, the voice of God was going to speak to him. It was a clear ocular demonstration of "hearing from God." Numbers 7:89 says:

> **When Moses entered the tent of meeting to speak with the Lord, he heard the voice speaking to him from between the two cherubim above the atonement cover on the ark of the covenant law. In this way the Lord spoke to him.**

This is going to sound simple and yet it is probably one of the most profound things that could be communicated to a Christian. It is important that along with your worship and witness, your service and your sacrifice, your offerings, and obedience, you be able to hear from God. The practice of prayer as a mere activity is not as important as why you surrender to that practice: to hear from God. The direction of your life and the transformation of your thoughts, the mapping of your life, and the processing of your considerations, all depend on whether or not you can hear from God. The distinction between theology and spirituality is most clearly illustrated here. If theology is talking about God, and spirituality the practice of the presence of God, then I would much rather hear from God than be able to describe or communicate the practice of "hearing."

The wonder and conversation of faith these days is unfortunately weighted on the side of commentary while being anemic on the side of communicating with God. You need to be able to hear from God. In the absence of a Tent of Meeting, how do you hear from God? Certainly, we hear from God through our engagement with the Word of God, which is the disclosed will of God. I cannot stress enough that the Bible was not written as much for the practice of faith as it was for the sharing of the reality of God, the revelation of the will of God, and the promises extended to those that would follow God. We hear from God through His Word.

We hear from Him by the Spirit of God that dwells inside of us, who reminds us, inspires us, and interprets for us what He has said and where He is moving, and the meaning of God's movement in and around our lives is divinely imagined and purpose-driven.

We hear from God, thirdly, through a communicator of spiritual truth—meaning, our faith is jarred from dormancy by hearing the Word when it is preached.

If you know your life is best lived when hearing from God, then you know what things ought to dominate your time and attention more than anything else. We live in a world of excessive commentary. It is often bereft of first-source material. We hear speculation, guessing about motives, and intentions. Our lives are too special; our time here is too short to live on anything less than first-source material. It is simple to believe that since God is the eternal Creator of everything, then God is first-source accurate when it comes to my life and the decisions that need to be made regarding it. Therefore, I want more than mere commentary about His will; I want to hear from God concerning His will for my life and His work manifested all around me every day.

Moses went into the Tent of Meeting and heard the voice of God. I want to suggest that hearing from God is much simpler than we often consider. Moses taught that hearing from God is an:

- **Intentioned pursuit. Moses in his interactions with the people had to have portions of a day or periods in a season when he stopped leading and listening to the voices of the people. He would go in that tent so he could hear from God. Part of his privilege to hear from God was simply making the intentioned effort to *go into the tent*. It marked a pulling away from the leading, a separation from the people, a silencing from the noise—and I am sure positioning his life in this way opened him to hear.**

- **Involved practice. This tent was built for nothing but the practice of the presence of God. It was** prioritized so much that Moses had it constructed and only housed in it what facilitated that practice-nothing else. There could be no confusion about what took place in it and no distraction once in it. What have you built in your life, either your internal spaces or your external spaces, that when you are there, you cannot be stirred for anything but hearing from God? One of the reasons I rise so early is because nothing is competing with my time with God. At no other point in the day does God get my direct attention as He does long before most of the world awakens. The suggestion I am making is, if you want to hear from God in your life, then build space in your life intentionally for that, so you are never confused about the priority that hearing from God should have in your life.

- Interested pursuit. Do you know one of the most effective ways to hear from God? Be interested in hearing from Him. I know that sounds a little sarcastic, but I am serious. The fragility of many people's prayer lives and spiritual practices is the misconception that God needs to hear more of what is on your mind than you need to hear what is on His mind. Hearing from God

presupposes that you think it is more important to listen than to be heard. The stronger part of communication has never been in the talking but in the listening. Strong listeners are far more effective communicators than eloquent and skilled speakers. Hearing from God is made all the easier when you want to hear from Him.

Today, wrestle with the question and be changed by the exercise of wrestling: In your life, is it more important that you hear from God or that you tell God how you are feeling? What are you thinking about and where you are emotionally? How are you interpreting things in and around your life? Is it more important that you hear God's will for you or that you confirm whether God thinks your will is in line with His purposes? Do you want to know if God will bless what you are thinking or would you like for God to tell you what God is thinking?

I am not at all suggesting that God is disinterested in what you are thinking and the decisions you are pondering. I am not saying that what is on your mind is not important and that you do not have critical decisions to make, because clearly, you do. I would never suggest that we do not need a conversation about our interpretation of what God's Word has said and what it possibly means.

I enjoy listening to CNN, FOX, MSNBC, the BBC, and other television stations because they each bring an intentional slant to their reporting of the news. It is healthy and opens considerations, broadens and deepens debate, but for matters of the soul, I need to hear from God more than I need to dump on Him.

If you ever want to see me visibly irritated, then watch me be involved in a conversation where someone is outtalking the expert about their field of expertise or signaling that there was no interest in what the expert says about a given matter. If I am asked about something and before I can comment regarding it a person starts telling me their opinion about it, then I have developed the practice of disengaging because there is no sense in me competing against the entertainment they are providing for themselves.

If there is a critical and vital need in your time of difficulty, then I cannot think of one stronger than your need to hear from God. Make it your pursuit. Become committed to the practice and treat it like a priority because God is always speaking with an eternity of things to share.

QUESTIONS FOR THOUGHT

1. What are some ways you can clear your mind and vicinity of distractions that prevent you from hearing from God?

2. How can you be more intentional about setting aside time to "go to the Tent of Meeting," so to speak, or make an appointment for listening to the Lord?

3. If you are honest with yourself, then would you say that you are not as interested in hearing what God has to say as you should be?

LET US PRAY

Lord, we confess today that we have often thought it more important to unload what we are thinking and feeling rather than to listen to what Your heart wants to share. Forgive us for wanting to say more than we are willing to hear. I pray that You would meet us in the Tent of Meeting we construct in our hearts and minds that separates us from the world and quiets us from the noise and focuses us on nothing but listening to your voice. We are literally in awe of You for wanting to speak to us, and equally in awe of the depth to which You speak to us.

May we meet You often and listen attentively because our current times and circumstances confirm that we need to hear from You. We need words from You, because if we do not hear from You, then what shall we do? We do want You more each day. Tell us and show us Your perfect way; there is no other way that we can live! In Jesus' name, we pray. Amen.

DAY 12 MEDITATION

WAITING FOR NEXT TIME

I am sure Noah built the ark wondering if his faith had been properly connected to God since he was building when there had been no significant rain on the earth. I suppose Noah would have felt more assured about it if he not been the only one building. Nonetheless, Noah followed his stirred faith and built the ark as God commanded.

The reward for Noah, I suspect, was when that door of the ark is closed. Having collected his family and a male and female of every living thing on the earth, Noah heard the release of the waters that had been held in the heavens. The water crashed to the earth for forty straight days. Noah had to be deeply grateful to have been selected to be spared from and delivered to the other side of this flood.

I can imagine that Noah had to be anxious to see what life would look like after the flood. After forty days, the floodwaters finally stopped. All of creation was flooded. With every living being destroyed, the floating future of the earth was shut up in that ark, waiting to see what God would do. For 150 days, the flood continued to cover the earth until, the text says, "God remembered Noah."

That line suggests that at the moment, God started letting the waters slowly recede. When Noah finally saw mountain peaks for the first time since God shut the door of the ark, Scripture informs us that he sent out a raven and observed. Noah used the raven to detect whether there was anything outside of the ark that was no longer underwater. Noah noticed that the raven flashed to and fro, finding no place to rest.

After Noah watched the raven, he sends out a dove. The dove returned having found not one place to perch outside of the ark. When the dove returned, Noah opened the window, brought it back inside, and shut the window. Noah then waited seven more days before releasing that dove again. The dove still not finding a place to perch, returned to the ark. But this time the dove returned with a leaf in its beak.

Noah now had to wait seven additional days. Once again, Noah released that dove. This time, we learned, the dove did not return. Noah removed the covering from the ark and notices that the earth is completely dry.

We know that Noah felt grateful to have been selected to survive when he was shut-in. Noah had to feel equally, if not more, grateful to have survived and to see the reward of his obedient faith. We know how Noah felt prior to the waters being released. This requires no guessing. Noah was relieved that he had spent his life obeying God, concerned about his future, wondering about whether he was able to manage the unknown.

We know how Noah felt during the long days while the rains poured down. Noah carried on his shoulders the weight of the entire survival of every living creature on the earth, wondering to himself how long it would last.

We know also how Noah felt when he finally emerged from the ark for the first time after the waters receded. Again, this requires no speculating. Noah was humbled that he was selected. Noah was hopeful about the future. He lived in awe of the power of God. Noah had to be elated that he was finally moving toward the unknown future, anticipating the days to come. Noah had to be worshipful of the God whose anger lasts for a moment, but whose mercy extends for a lifetime.

So we know how Noah must have felt going into the ark. We know how Noah must have felt emerging from the ark. But what strikes me is the number of days in between—the days that Noah had to manage the disappointment of seeing the raven fly without finding a resting perch and knowing that it was not time yet. After so many days, weeks, and months of anxiety, releasing the dove and then having to open that window to bring that same dove back in and wait seven more days—what was Noah thinking and feeling in that in-between time?

When the dove returned with the leaf in its beak, Noah was prevented from moving towards a life on the other side of this ark and flood season, what was he feeling? To have released the dove a final time, wait to see if it would come back, what was Noah thinking? How did Noah handle the repeated letdowns as symbolized by the patterns, the movements, the activities of a raven and a dove?

I imagine in your season of hardship that you have been hit repeatedly with the reality that you have to offer God another "seven days," so to speak—another period of waiting.

Noah survived forty days of unrelenting waters released from the heavens, followed by 150 days of floating on the waters of the unknown. You would think that the last series of seven days, in which he sends out the raven and the dove, would have been more than enough to make him lose faith in whatever was supposed to happen next.

But the lesson of this text is that what God is going to do in your future is worth the repeated attempts to move forward. Faith always believes in the "next time."

God has a "next time" in your life. "Next time" is why Noah was able to send that dove out after the raven was unsuccessful. When Noah had to open the window and let that dove back in, he did not hesitate. Noah retrieved it and waited another seven days. Then Noah opened the window again and repeated the cycle. Why? Because Noah never lost faith in the gift and possibility of a "next time."

Thank God that Noah did not give up. Even though Noah must have been frustrated from all the time he had been locked into that ark, he believed it was worth trying again. Noah decided that no matter how many times that dove returned, he would give it time and then make another attempt.

Every time life does something to make you shut that window because what you thought was next is not happening today, I need you to trust God enough that you will decide, "I don't care how long I have to wait; when it's my turn to show up, I'm going to show up and believe that if it didn't happen before, it can happen now."

Consider the unsuccessful attempts of your past. What will you do differently next time? How will you think differently next time? What will you say? How slow will you be to move? What counsel will you seek? What patience will you exercise? What prayers will you offer? What apology will you ask for? What forgiveness will you extend? What mercy will you display? What dream will you hold tighter? Whatever those questions are, try to answer them in ways that honor God and demonstrate your faith.

The dove returning and the raven searching for a perch and not being able to find it. These are not signs of "never." There is a "next time." The best offering you can give to God is to keep that window open for "not right now" and to let it rest with you for just a little while longer. Treat it right and steward it faithfully, because a "next time" is coming.

In your time of uncertainty and anxiety be comforted by the fact that God remembers you. You are not alone in this period of difficulty. You are not forgotten by the Lord. The capsule that you feel so confined by may be buoying you and bringing you to the place that you need to be in your life to begin a new season.

So do not despair. Your waiting will not be for always. God remembers you.

QUESTIONS FOR THOUGHT

1. In this season of difficulty that you are in, have you seen timelines extended and waiting periods drawn out? Are there milestones you expected to pass or hopes that left you disappointed?

2. How does the thought of Noah waiting in that ark and the knowledge of his eventual release from it, give you hope for your future?

3. Even if your current time of suffering or pain were to last until the end of your life on Earth, then what promises are waiting for you in Heaven as a child of God?

LET US PRAY

Lord, today we bow at the foot of the cross to wait on You and to give You our trust in these troubled times. We do not know when You are going to let us open the window to this ark we are in. We have no idea when the floodwaters are going to recede. We do not know when trouble is going to subside, but we know You are the same yesterday, today, and forever. With how faithful You have been to us seven days ago, and the seven days before that, can we not give You seven more days before we release our dove? If the dove returns and we have got to deal with trouble again next week, and deal with the emotional struggle, and deal with disappointment, then we are prepared to release our dove again and again, because we know that You are working even when we do not see it.

The Bible tells us that while we are waiting, we can be of good courage, because if we can wait on You, then You will strengthen our hearts. We recognize that when You created us, You also gave us the capacity to endure the things You would place in our path. If our "next time" is not today, next week, next year, or even in this life, then we will continue to wait on You, knowing that You will neither leave us nor forsake us. We thank You and we love You for it. In Jesus' name, we pray. Amen.

DAY 13 MEDITATION

JESUS AS FRIEND

How do people generally understand what it means to be a Christian? To adhere to a certain set of rules? To act nicer than people who claim no attachment to Christianity? To be docile in society, quiet about issues of justice and fairness? To be depended upon to comply with society's rules and to focus on the sweet afterlife of eternity with God?

Yet, being a Christian is to have accepted an invitation extended by God to live one's life by faith in the redeeming work of Jesus, who laid down His life to atone for humanity's sins and bring us into the right relationship with God. That is first. The second is to live out Christ's life in you manifested in your relationships with other people, highlighted by service and with the display of spiritual fruit: love, joy, peace, forbearance, kindness, goodness, faithfulness, gentleness, and self-control. Paul teaches that we are known to be Christian by the fruit we bear.

I was fifteen years old when my music teacher bought me a pocket-sized New Testament. I can still remember the initial excitement of reading what was assigned to me, which was the Gospel of John. Despite my excitement, I was immediately frustrated that I had entered into my search to understand God through the wrong door. I entered through the door of rules and regulations, searching for dos and don'ts. I saw the Bible and my engagement with it as a guidebook for living in pursuit of rewards. I saw it as a rule book for behavior with the weightiest part of that being to avoid wrong behavior. Every page was a reminder of how far I was from living out God's will on Earth. The Book of John teaches:

> **Greater love has no one than this: to lay down one's life for one's friends. You are my friends if you do what I command. I no longer call you servants, because a servant does not know his master's business. Instead, I have called you friends, for everything that I learned from my Father I have made known to you. (John 15:13-15).**

I can remember being as struck by the image then as I am stirred by it now. Jesus calls me *friend!* It was the idea that maybe being a Christian starts with accepting the invitation to salvation but immediately is also understood as a life's friendship with Jesus. Have you ever envisioned that this is what it means to be a Christian for you? To live in friendship with Jesus. This friendship means the Lord has value-driven affection for you, which means His love for you is not based upon your behavior or reciprocity but on His choice. Jesus considers you a friend because He chooses to. You cannot earn it. The friendship of Jesus cannot be measured in blessings or burdens; it just is.

It is generally easier to communicate with friends. There is an excitement about anticipating spending time with friends. I tend to listen attentively to friends and want to respond to the needs of friends. I trust the critique of friends. I know in battle who fights alongside me. I make sacrifices for friends. At this stage of my life, I do not shelve my authentic self when around my friends; I let friends into my sacred space. I rejoice and hurt with and for friends.

I wonder if when thinking about what it means to be a Christian, whether you have developed a conviction around Jesus as a friend. It does not eliminate His want for us to walk being led by the Spirit. It does not eliminate His wanting us to break free from privilege and to see life through the experiences of people not like us so that we can respond to human need.

So, what does it mean to be a Christian? It means to nurture the friendship Jesus extends to you and not just to exist around people, not just to tolerate people, but to do the hard work of seeking friendship with others around you. My job is to not expect people to step up into space I occupy, but for me to step down into the spaces where people are—people I need to be connected to for the advancement of Jesus' vision of collective friendship. This is precisely what Jesus did for us in the incarnation; He stepped down to relate to us.

If you are a Christian, then you are nurturing a friendship with Jesus and developing friendships with others, including those who are not like you. One of the greatest honors of my life was to fly to Vegas to marry my friend Chip to his fiancée. I met Chip on a golf trip where I was the only one in the group who was staying one extra day and thus forced to play golf with two white guys who were strangers. We started as most would, cautious and dancing around each other conversationally until they found out I was a preacher. My new friends became fascinated with what they thought was a strange combination of golf and preaching. We had a ball during our round of golf. When we shook hands on the 18th green, Chip went in his pocket and gave me his business card, which was something mirroring a casino gambling chip.

Chip then said, "Reverend, it's been real cool, and if you are ever in Vegas, call me and let's play around." I thanked him and his buddy and put the chip in my golf bag. Weeks later, when preaching on a Sunday in Los Angeles I was asked to stay to preach on Tuesday. The pastor suggested that Sunday night we fly to Vegas and enjoy Eddie Griffin's stand-up, hang out in Vegas on Monday all day, and return to L.A. Tuesday morning. I remembered that chip in my bag and asked the pastor if he would mind if I played golf on Monday. I called Chip and he picked me up. We played golf all day Monday. We talked, laughed, and compared notes of our racial experiences.

Months later, I called Chip and asked him to fly to Pittsburgh to play in our church golf tournament. Chip did. He had a chance to hang out with friends of mine. I never will forget the phone call months later when Chip wanted to tell me he had proposed to his fiancée.

Even though his fiancée had never met me, Chip wanted me to fly to Vegas to perform their ceremony. I consented. I flew out the day before and played golf with him and his white and Italian friends. Like me introducing him at our golf tournament as my brother, with no other explanation attached, so he did the same with his friends. Each respective crowd looked at us both, trying to see the resemblance, and then decided that if we were not explaining it, then they were not asking.

The highlight for me was on the night of the wedding. In the frantic attempt to get everybody in place on time, Chip asked, "Dude, I need your help." He was holding a tie in his hand and said, "How do I do that tie knot like you have?" We found a mirror and tied his tie. Then his father comes up and says, "Hey, Reverend, I want a knot like yours too." The only black man was treated like the frantically pushed rest of the family, all helping each other get ready. When the wedding started, I wish you could have seen the faces of guests who were wondering why I was standing at the front, alone, suited and smiling at an all-white and Italian wedding. Later at the reception, Chip introduced me, "I want to thank my brother for coming." We both looked out at people as if to let them figure it out.

It forced others to come over and ask how we met. The guys I had played golf with earlier, who have also invited wedding guests, invited me on a golf trip they do at another point in the year. I did not fly out there because of our skin color; I flew out there because of our friendship, knowing our skin color would provide suspicion and speculation for others.

Do you know what being a Christian looks like? It looks like friendship. This is what the Lord wants with you. Don't get us mired in the search for how to pray, how to hear from God, how to find your calling, how to know when you are led by the Spirit. Each of these is important—but nurture the friendship you have with Jesus and these other things will reveal themselves.

Nurture friendship with others too. I guess you know what I am pushing: we cannot fix a race problem bunkered to protect our forts of suspicion while others stay hidden behind their walls of privilege. We both perish from the bankrupt life we live not experiencing each other.

If you are a Christian, then Jesus expects you to aim for different goals than the world aims for—one being friendship. Even friendship with those viewed as enemies. How is that possible? It's precisely what God did for us. When you say, "But that's God," I respond, "Yes, and you are the expression of God in the Earth, so go and do thou likewise."

> **I've told you these things for a purpose: that my joy might be your joy, and your joy wholly mature. This is my command: Love one another the way I loved you. This is the very best way to love. Put your life on the line for your friends. You are my friends when you do the things I command you. I'm no longer calling you servants because servants don't understand what their master is thinking and planning. No, I've named you friends because I've let you in on everything I've heard from the Father. (John 15:11-15 MSG).**

QUESTIONS FOR THOUGHT

1. Has your current hardship brought you in contact with new people or made you more sensitive to the perspective of someone different from you?

2. Have you ever considered friendship to be one of your goals or missions during this difficult time?

3. Have you experienced an "unlikely" friendship in the past? If so, then what has it taught you about God?

LET US PRAY

Lord, thank You that You do not just call us disciples; You call us friends. You demonstrated your friendship by laying down Your life for us. Help us to demonstrate that same friendship for others, including those with whom we differ and even see as enemies. Show us Your strength to let love prevail.

May all of us lay our privilege at the altar, may all of us lay our suffering at the altar, and may we see what life looks like when all is amassed for the common good. We saw this in the early church, so we know it is possible. My prayer is that You will make us the remnant in this culture that reflects Your will on Earth as it is in Heaven. In Jesus' name, we pray. Amen.

DAY 14 MEDITATION

JOURNALING YOUR JOURNEY

Today, spend time in prayer and reflection on what you have digested in this week's meditations. Record your thoughts, emotions, insights, and prayers on the following pages. "Journaling your journey" through this difficult time in your life not only serves to help you process your experience at the moment but will be something you can look back on in the future as evidence of how God has worked in your life.

_____

_____

_____

_____

Day 14 Meditation: Journaling Your Journey

_____

_____

_____

_____

_____

_____

_____

_____

_____

_____

_____

_____

_____

_____

_____

_____

_____

_____

_____

_____

_____

_____

Day 14 Meditation: Journaling Your Journey

_____

_____

_____

_____

_____

_____

_____

_____

_____

_____

_____

DAY 15 MEDITATION

GOD'S WILL MUST CONTROL YOUR LIFE

J.I. Packer, a thoughtful Canadian-born theologian, said that once you become aware that the main business you are here for is to know God, then most of life's problems fall into place of their own accord. How do you know the will of God for your life? How do you leave family and friends to let God lead you up a mountain where, upon arrival, you are to kill your only son as a sacrifice in obedience to what you believe He has led you to do? How do you accept an anointing for a throne that you will have to wait before occupying when so much of the waiting will involve deep battles that will leave lasting scars? How do you leave a great paying job and accept a position in another place by following the unction of the Spirit nudging your decisions? One of the hardest and most mysterious considerations regarding our faith is to discern how to know the will of God.

When you pray and read Scripture, the flood of options, thoughts, and imaginations come rushing in, how do you discriminate between what is your natural passion? What do you think is the logical choice, or even the voices of people you respect and admire? What do you believe is the will of God? This is one of the hardest things to confirm. It can be frustrating to be caught needing to make a critical decision and standing at the intersection of multiple options, with several of them equal in benefit or equal in sacrifice, and not know what represents the will of God.

Ephesians chapter 5 has as one of its themes developing obedience around the example of Christ. Paul is teaching that imitating Christ is our chief aim, not only in our spiritual considerations but also in our daily human interactions.

To intimately connect to His life, and then seek to imitate it, is the sure desire of every Christian. Jesus' steps are so sure and His words so precise because He was never outside of the will of God. Paul, in chapter 5, is laying out what distinguishes a Christian. Among all of that Paul includes in verse 17, which reads like this:

"Therefore do not be foolish, but understand what the Lord's will is." *The Message* Translation says: "Don't live carelessly, unthinkingly. Make sure you understand what the Master wants."

I do not want to detour but it ought to be said that our faith in Christ is a thinking person's exchange. You do not only feel your way through your spirituality; you have to, more importantly, think your way through it. We love God with what? Body, soul, and mind! We are told what the Lord's aim is in your life: to transform you by the renewing of your mind. God wants you to think.

As certain as the instruction is, the struggle of knowing God's will is real. Especially when you are considering life-altering decisions. Our decisions are so critical: career choices, love, and relationships, and sometimes as difficult as determining how long someone stays on a ventilator as opposed to letting them pass to life eternal. When should I stop pressing or fighting, or when should I push harder and wait longer for doors I believe the Lord has set in place for me? How do I know when I am being pushed or pulled by God or when I am merely being pushed or pulled by my frustration and fatigue? How do I know the will of God?

- It starts with a pursuit to purely know God. Understanding His will comes as you become so close to Him that His will is natural to your thought process. Your faith is, first and foremost, about a relationship with the Lord. Relationships have authentic love and open communication along with the want for mutual happiness. People who spend a lot of time with me will say this: so-and-so asked me if I thought you would be interested in considering this venture or joining in on this opportunity and I told them, "I'll ask him, but I know he will probably not go with that" or "I'll ask him, but I know he will say yes to that." They did not hear me say yes, but they know me so well that they know why and how I shape my "yeses" and my "no's". We want to know God so well that it is easy to interpret His will because we read about His character, spend so much time with Him in prayer, worship in His presence, and enjoy conversation about Him with others so much that when we decide between decisions and opinions, it is easier to discern which one represents His will. So the question is: What are you doing? What disciplines are you practicing? What is the level of your want to nurture your relationship with God? It should be reflected in your devotional life, your prayer life, and your worship life.

- There has to be a willingness to submit to being guided. Do you know how many people want to know God's will but do not want to follow any decision unless it is the decision they want to make? Surrender to being led and do not accept that all the responsibility for your decisions is on you. Those decisions are too heavy for you to carry on your own. I have a simple prayer I pray when I know the decision is critical: "Lord, only open the door towards the direction that you want me to walk through and please close all other doors because I am too confused to distinguish." I am appealing to God to guide me. Then I can move naturally with wherever God is opening the door. God has never let me walk through a wrong door. If you want to live your life knowing God's will, then submit now to being willing to be led.

- Be intentional about exercising your discernment. Discernment means the ability to distinguish. While it is a deep spiritual word, to every one of us a measure of discernment has been given. Do you know that spiritual gifts, as well as spiritual disciplines, need exercise too? You can be extremely gifted. However, if you do not nurture that gift, then it will always be an uncomfortable flow when it is at work in your life. If you want to know the will of God, then you must nurture your discernment. Try making discerning judgments about things and check your accuracy. Admit when you missed it. Learn from it, so it becomes natural to your life. Then, when you most vitally need it, it will not let you down. Here is what you in faith have to believe: God is not hiding His will. God wants you to know His will. God wants me to know what He desires for me and how He expects me to embrace, manage, and nurture my decisions with His will being predominant. God is not trying to hide it from me or make me jump through unnecessary hoops to make obedient decisions. What biblical character can you point to who asked God to disclose His will and God made it a game of hide and seek? For life-altering decisions, God wants you to know His will. Listen to what Paul says in Romans 12:2: "So do not conform to the pattern of this world, but be transformed by the renewing of your mind. Then you will be able to test and approve what God's will is—his good, pleasing and perfect will." That word conform means to have the same pattern as the world or to be shaped by the world. Instead, we are already shaped by God and have the same pattern as Him. So we do not need to be conformed. We only need to be transformed, which means to be changed after being with Him. I need to be changed after being with God and then I can know His will.

A.W. Tozer said: "God has not bowed to our nervous haste nor embraced the methods of our machine age. The man who would know God must give time to Him."

George Truitt said: "Success is knowing God's will and being right in the center of it."

Writing about God's sure guidance, British Pastor Frank W. Boreham recounted a time when a minister visited his home in New Zealand. Being young and inexperienced, Boreham sought the counsel of his guest. Boreham said that one morning they were sitting on the veranda, looking out over the golden plains to the purple sunlit mountains. Boreham asked the minister, "Can a man be sure that in the hour of perplexity he will be rightly led by God? Can he feel secure against making a false step?"

"I am certain of it," exclaimed the minister, "if he will but give God time! As long as you live, remember that. Give God time!"

If you seek the Will of God, then God will honor it by making sure you do not miss it. It is what Jesus teaches: "Seek the Kingdom of God above all else, and live righteously, and He will give you everything you need". (Matthew 6:33 NLT).

Paul prayed that you would know God's will when he said in Colossians 1:9-10:

> **We ask God to give you complete knowledge of His will and to give you spiritual wisdom and understanding. Then the way you live will always honor and please the Lord, and your lives will produce every kind of good fruit. All the while, you will grow as you learn to know God better and better. (NLT).**

You can know the will of God. I want you to not be ashamed of searching for His will and to let others know that you are not moving until His will is made manifest to you. When God bolts the door, do not try to get in through the window. The will of God will never lead you where the grace of God cannot keep you.

The struggle of knowing the will of God is often illuminated by the number of voices you allow to influence your life. You can talk to too many people. You can highly regard too many people's opinions until you think yourself right out of the will of God. Instead, choose that there is no greater spiritual desire you could ever have than to know what God's will is for your life.

QUESTIONS FOR THOUGHT

1. Have you struggled with knowing how God's will could include your current time of pain, difficulty, waiting, or suffering?

2. What is God's will for your life at this moment?

3. Are you willing to allow God full control of your life, both now and in the future?

LET US PRAY

Lord, we come in Jesus' name to thank You for being gracious enough to reveal Your will to us, loving enough to not want us to live without knowing what Your will is, and forgiving enough to not disqualify us for moving outside of Your will to date. Today, we pray that Your will would be made plain to us, that our spiritual disciplines will have put us in a place where we don't have to wrestle with what Your will is. We can be bold enough to trust Your will if and when it is second-guessed by those around us. We are Your sheep, we know Your voice, and another we will not follow. When the decisions are critical or we feel crunched by time, and pressed in the need to decide, please remove every barrier and destroy every competitive high place constructed in our lives to confuse us about what Your perfect will is for our lives.

We do not even want to breathe without Your will. We will submit to letting Your will lead, no matter what. You promised to walk with us and to be with us until the end of this age and we rest our very lives on that. Make us unashamed when we have to tell people we are waiting to hear from You. Calm our anxiety when time is pressing You into a decision for which You feel no rush. Grant us peace as we wait to confirm what Your will is for our lives. We ask it in Jesus' name. Amen.

DAY 16 MEDITATION

POOR IN SPIRIT

Much of Matthew chapter 5 has been used directly in the teaching of the early church as it fought to discern what it meant to be a follower of the risen Christ. There was an early fascination with creating a linkage between Jesus and Moses. Jesus was by many believed to be the New Moses, and Matthew highlighted it.

In Matthew 5, we have what is referred to as the Beatitudes, which are teachings on how to live a blessed life. The parallelism between Jesus and Moses started here because, when Jesus saw a crowd He went up onto a mountain like Moses, who upon ascent was given the law. But Jesus sat down, taking the posture of a rabbi, and His disciples drew close. There Jesus began to teach them. He did not teach them about institutional responsibility or social responsibility. Jesus started by teaching them how to order the interior of their lives to live a happy, fortunate, and blessed life.

What Jesus taught, and the fact that He gives this protracted teaching session is a reminder to us that amidst all the swirling social engagement and conversation taking place around us that begs our attention. It cannot be to the negation of the continual work that must take place in the interior life. Jesus ascended the mountain and assumed His seat as rabbi. We gather around Him as He taught. What did Jesus teach first?

Blessed are the poor in spirit, for theirs is the kingdom of heaven. (Matthew 5:3).

Imagine that you are alone in the presence of Jesus, upon seeing your countenance and sensing your fatigue, He asks you what is wrong. You begin to tell Him all about your struggles and difficulties in this hard time. Jesus smiles and bids you sit with Him. Jesus says, "Let Me tell you the path to spiritual blessedness. This is what we call the Beatitudes." His first teaching is: you are blessed when you approach your spirituality poor in spirit.

St. Gregory of Nyssa, a mystic who lived in Cappadocia, described the Beatitudes this way:

> **Beatitude is a possession of all that's held to be good, from which nothing is absent that good desire may want. Perhaps the meaning of beatitude may become clearer to us if it is compared with its opposite. The opposite of beatitude is misery. Misery means being afflicted unwillingly with painful sufferings.**

We might, after that description, want to listen to what Jesus is teaching. What does Jesus mean when He says, "You will live blessed when you are poor in Spirit"? It is as if He says, "You are fortunate when living in the reality of little to no outward support and you instead value inward dependence on God." It is to live humble with the realization that all your gifts and blessings come from the grace of God. It suggests that one lives empty and open to the Word of God.

The biblical, historical, and theological understanding of this goes like this: you are fortunate when because of sustained economic privation and social distress, you have confidence *only* in God. This does not mean that there is a lack of concern for the materially poor because it is to the materially poor that Jesus said He was directing the focus of His mission on Earth. What it does mean is God will use our inability to address our social chasms as a way of birthing humility in people who will find themselves dependent on Him.

Jesus wants you to spiritually live to discern the futility of the external world that so many become fixated on. Owning things and having experiences is great. You should aspire to and prioritize them, but not more than what ought to be a continual focus on the blessings that come from living dependent on God. This means that you can be monetarily blessed and still be spiritually dependent on the Lord. You can have seasonal peace and still be dependent on the Lord, as long as these things do not have space in your life where you depend on them for your identity, emotional health, or relational connections. This is what Jesus meant when He said, "You are fortunate if you live poor in spirit."

Listen to Terry Laughlin describe His understanding of this verse:

> **To be poor in spirit is not poverty-stricken, financially poor or having a lack of courage. It is a spiritual poverty, acknowledging our utter dependence upon God for our spiritual needs, knowing that our spiritual needs and even all of our mental and physical needs can only be truly**

satisfied through a vibrant personal relationship with Jesus Christ.

The poor in spirit realize that they are unable to respond to life's trials and temptations in a way that is pleasing to God unless He enables them to be overcomers.

An anonymous author shares this about Matthew 5:3:

My guess is that few if any would understand the tremendous promise of such a statement. To be stripped bare, forsaken and rejected, is a blessing? How can such deprivation be of any good, let alone a blessing? Perhaps that would be difficult under the circumstances. Nevertheless, as I was watching the evening news the other day, I did find one old lady who knew it well. The camera caught her wading chest deep in the murky waters of a flooded New Orleans street. The reporter yelled out to her, "How are you? Where are you going?" She simply replied, "I got my life and I got my Jesus. The rest don't matter." The moment was probably lost on the reporter and many of those listening in. Nevertheless, to the Christian, it ought to have rung true and clear. If we have life and faith, everything else is a dividend, a blessing we can hope for but ought never count on.

I know you want to be happy and live, fortunately. The question is, what would be the ease or the difficulty in developing a dependence on God that makes everything else superfluous?

- It depends on where you have placed the Lord in your hierarchy of needs.

- It tests and sifts just how much you depend on other things.

- It invites you to change where you search for fulfillment.

Paul found it in Philippians 4:10-13:

I rejoiced greatly in the Lord that at last you renewed your concern for me. Indeed, you were concerned, but you had no opportunity to show it. I am not saying this because I am in need, for I have learned to be content whatever the circumstances. I know what it is to be in need, and I know what it is to have plenty. I have learned the secret of being content in any and every situation, whether well fed or hungry, whether living in plenty or in want. I can do all this through him who gives me strength.

Did you hear that "poor in spirit" testimony? He said, I am not able to live on either side of life's realities unless it's through God; it's a total dependency.

Several years ago, a newspaper in Greensboro, North Carolina, carried a story about a tractor-trailer rolling along on a side street in a southern city. The driver came to a low bridge and misjudged the height of his rig. When the truck came to a stop, it was wedged tightly between the bridge and the street. Wreckers were called to remove the truck, but with all of their skills and equipment, they could not budge it. Among the bystanders was a young student. The lad walked over to the men and suggested that the tires on the truck be deflated. As the air screamed from the tires, the truck began to settle slowly away from the bridge. A wrecker was chained to the truck and it was gently pulled backward. When the truck was free of the bridge, the tires were reinflated, and the trucker was again on his way.

Tell me you are not shouting over the clarity of that kind of illustration. The Lord is teaching that you are so fortunate when you can let the air of arrogance, entitlement, and self-occupation out of the tires that feed your ego and let God pull you from tight spots so you can be free to move about happy and fulfilled. The revelation of one's closeness to the Lord Jesus can be measured in the depth to which one is dependent upon God. To be so dependent that regular conversations with God are required for your spiritual and emotional health, so dependent that you cannot get through a conversation without calling His name, so dependent that to have everything stripped from you but Jesus makes you feel like the most fortunate person on the planet. Blessed are the poor in spirit because the kingdom is suited for them.

QUESTIONS FOR THOUGHT

1. Has your current trial helped to make you poorer in spirit than you were before it began?

2. Do arrogance, entitlement, and self-occupation often dominate your thoughts and attitudes? How do you combat those traits?

3. Why do you think contentment is such a difficult practice to master?

LET US PRAY

Lord, thank You that Your work in us is never only for our external worlds, and You are so acutely aware of what our real needs are. Only You know all the needs of our interior lives because You made us, and You fill our lives with Your Spirit. Help us to live our lives as You have taught: the poor in spirit, always living to reflect our helpless dependence on You. May that become a witness to others until we all can deflate these egos, defeat this pride, and walk with You in true humility, seeing the needs in others and sacrificing our lives for the common good. We trust Your every teaching and surrender to align our lives in obedience to the same. We pray in Jesus' name. Amen.

DAY 17 MEDITATION

GROWING THROUGH MOURNING

A young pastor visited Dundee, Scotland, shortly after Robert Murray M'Cheyne died at the age of thirty. Many people had come to Christ because of M'Cheyne's ministry. The visitor wanted to know the secret of his great influence.

The old sexton of M'Cheyne's church led the preacher into the rectory and showed him some books lying on a table. Then the sexton motioned to the chair the evangelist had used and said, "Sit down and put your elbows on the table." The visitor obeyed. "Now put your head in your hands." The visitor complied. "Now let the tears flow; that's what M'Cheyne did."

Next, the sexton led him into the church and said, "Put your elbows on the pulpit." The visitor obeyed by placing his elbows on the pulpit. "Now put your face in your hands." Again, the pastor obeyed. "Now let the tears flow; that's what M'Cheyne used to do."

Robert Murray M'Cheyne cried freely over his sins and those of his people. By contrast, our emotions are often hardened toward sin. We need to be more sensitive to the convicting voice of God's Spirit and more determined to live a separated life. We may rejoice in God's forgiveness but we should never be afraid to mourn for our sins. Matthew 5:4 says,

> **Blessed are they who mourn: for they shall be comforted. (NKJV).**

To mourn means at its base to have a broken heart. In the Greek, to mourn means to have a deep inner pain that occurs when something tragic happens, such as the death of a loved one. It also means to have a desperate sorrow over evil and suffering. In this Scripture, it is mourning over sin against God and the results of it, which are spiritual death and eternal separation from God. It is a brokenness of heart that comes from understanding the suffering Christ went through upon the Cross and realizing that our sin put Him there.

What does God expect of us as it relates to our weaknesses and shortcomings, our sins, and our lives outside of the will of God? He expects us to mourn our lives, to lament, or feel regret about it. The sure sign that you are still sensitive to the Spirit is to regret the parts of your life not perfectly aligned to God's will.

God promises that you will be comforted. It means God will come to your aid.

Don't convince yourself that it is okay to not feel regret about walking staggered with God's will because when you stay in a posture of regret, God comes to your aid! How? God presents an alternative. God taps on your willpower and makes you see how much better your life would be without mourning or regretting your mark-missing when it comes to His will.

You will be comforted, which means the burden will be lifted. That reveals something about what regretting your mark-misses feels like. It is a weight to carry regret when you feel God pull but respond with a life that resists His pull. But you can experience a lifting of that weight by letting God come to your aid.

When I feel myself sinking in my head and cannot put my finger on it, I have learned it is because I am tired of carrying that extra weight. When I deal with God about it, He lightens the load, lifts my spirit, helps me to see the positives, and makes me less stressed about people's pull on my life.

Don't carry unnecessary weight because you have enough already.

- You are managing life through a tough season.

- You are negotiating relationships that are your assignment and not always your choice.

- You are responding to inner changes all the time and being invited to grow while the enemy tempts you to regress.

There are already enough weights in your life. I want you to hear the good news: God wants to come to your aid and lighten your load. All He needs is to sense that you carry evidence of regret about being off-centered about your relationship with Him.

The *Illustrated Bible Commentary* says this about this verse: "The loss of anything that a person counts valuable will produce mourning, whether it is one's financial support, loved ones, status in society, or even one's spiritual standing before God."

I try to shape my teaching to you in positive tones because I carry a conviction that good news is easier to embrace than bad news. It is not because I live untouched by the realities that hit our lives, but because we have the power to shape our realities by how we choose to think about them.

So here is the good news: wherever you are missing the center of God's will in your life, be inspired that God stands with you in it and wants to lighten that load for you if you can give Him evidence of regret about it.

If you regret missing God's mark in your life, then offer it to God. Don't ever settle, don't excuse it, don't let yourself convince yourself of anything less than God's perfect will for your life. Watch God come to your aid. You will know He has because you will feel like life is not as weighted as it was. Your mind and spirit will not be as heavy. Life will not be as stressful. Managing life will be easier.

The only survivor of a shipwreck washed up on a small, uninhabited island. He prayed feverishly for God to rescue him, and every day he scanned the horizon for help, but none seemed forthcoming. Exhausted, he eventually managed to build a

little hut out of driftwood to protect him from the elements and to store his few possessions.

But then one day, after scavenging for food, he arrived home to find his little hut in flames with the smoke rolling up to the sky. The worst had happened; everything was lost. He was stung with grief and anger. "God, how could you do this to me!" he cried.

Early the next day, however, he was awakened by the sound of a ship that was approaching the island. It had come to rescue him. "How did you know I was here?" asked the weary man of his rescuers.

"We saw your smoke signal," they replied.

One more story:

A man continually "rededicated" his life and always prayed the same prayer, "Lord, take the cobwebs out of my life. Oh, Lord...take the cobwebs out of my life!"

His pastor had heard this prayer more times than he cared to remember and was tired of hearing it. Finally, when the man uttered the prayer into his pastor's ear at the altar, "Lord, take the cobwebs out of my life," the pastor responded with a prayer of his own and yelled out, "Lord, don't take the cobwebs out...just kill the spider!"

Find the "spider" in your heart and then kill it. Turn away from your besetting sin that always trips you up. Real mourning over sin leads to real changes in our life. That is true repentance.

QUESTIONS FOR THOUGHT

1. Is there an unaddressed sin in your life that needs to be repented of and dealt with?

2. When is the last time you mourned over your sin?

3. Has your current time of difficulty brought you a new set of temptations and sins than you previously struggled with?

LET US PRAY

Lord, as we plan to walk through another day, sense our want to be as right in You as You desire. We love You so much and regret that we so consistently miss the mark of Your high calling in our lives. We think about it, emote it, and regret it. We often do not think about how much You help us even through our regrets, and so today we confess that we mourn living lives beneath Your will and accepting temptations that represent cheap alternatives to Your perfect design for our lives.

We are so strongly encouraged by how You come alongside us to lift the heavyweight of our regrets and sin. Our repentance today is our praise for the comfort You have delivered to each of our lives. Thank You for the lifting and for the lightness we feel in thought. As we go about our day, we are so grateful that we do so not weighed down by the sins that so easily beset us. We pray in the name of Jesus. Amen.

DAY 18 MEDITATION

STRONGER THROUGH MEEKNESS

Theologian and Trappist Monk Thomas Merton said: "Only when we are able to 'let go' of everything within us—all desire to see, to know, to taste, and to experience the presence of God—do we truly become able to experience that presence with the overwhelming conviction and reality that revolutionizes our entire inner life. Letting go in the moral order is the living out of the Beatitudes. In the order of prayer, it is in-depth *kenosis,* an emptying out of the contents of awareness so that one becomes oneself—an empty vessel, a broken vessel, a void that lies open before God and finds itself filled with God's own life."

Merton takes a long route to suggest that to live with "supreme blessedness," which is the definition of beatitude, to live a blessed life, there has to be an emptying of oneself to be filled in these emptied places by the presence of God. The purpose of our prayers, engagement with the Word, and true pursuit in worship is to shape lives that are always going through this emptying and filling experience. One of the ways I think about spiritual growth is to consider it in these terms. Every day I go through this emptying and filling process. This process covers the whole range of my life that includes my thinking, emotions, interactions, and disciplines. This process affects the way I see myself and the world around me, and my engagement with and understanding of God. Hear Jesus' teaching in Matthew 5:5 with this emptying and filling consideration:

Blessed are the meek, for they will inherit the earth.

Now, listen to it in the Amplified Version, which provides some wider description:

Blessed [inwardly peaceful, spiritually secure, worthy of respect] are the gentle [the kind-hearted, the sweet-spirited, the self-controlled], for they will inherit the earth.

If we apply our emptying and filling motif to this, then it would suggest that I am emptying myself of inward unsettledness, spiritual insecurity, and shame, to be filled with a kind heart, a pleasant spirit, and have learned how to master my emotions. The promise Jesus makes to us when this becomes our pursuit is that we will inherit the Earth.

Matthew is being apocalyptic about the promise because he is teaching that when Jesus comes back and ushers in the reign of Heaven on Earth as John reveals, it will be the meek that will inherit the fullness of whatever that reality will look like. That is a huge promise to those who pursue a life of meekness. So what does it mean?

Meekness is so opposite to our way of thinking these days because it describes a person who does not assert himself or herself over others to advance their causes. As you can tell, this defines how we relate to people. Meekness is not measuring the depth of prayer, energy in service, or quality of devotion to God. Meekness is measured by whether or not we can be our true selves around others without regarding them for the pursuit of our causes. Instead, can we be pleasant and emotionally controlled for the benefit of another, whom the Lord wants to impact by the offering of meekness we bring to the engagement? Can we be correct in the discussion, but not aggressive about forcing it, because God is using another person's belief that they have to be right to teach them of their weaknesses? Can you be pleasant in the face of tension for which your outburst would be the natural response, instead of letting the Lord use your meekness to impact the other person's life so they can see how desperately they need to draw closer to the Lord?

Jesus quotes Psalm 37:9-11, which says:

> **For evildoers shall be cut off: but those that wait upon the Lord, they shall inherit the earth. For yet a little while, and the wicked shall not be: yea, thou shalt diligently consider his place, and it shall not be. But the meek shall inherit the earth; and shall delight themselves in the abundance of peace. (KJV).**

Jesus is teaching that you cannot engage people for your cause and think that you will live a happy and fulfilled life. For Jesus, it was a political statement as much as it was defining personal exchanges. Not those who try to bring in the kingdom politically or militarily, but those who humbly wait on God will "inherit the earth" or "inherit the land."

It is making life about others and not yourself. I am shocked at some people I have to relate to who cannot see that whenever we talk, it is never about me and always about them.

I answered the phone and was excited: "Hey Bill, how are you?" We exchanged a few pleasantries and then it happened again: "Hey, what did you preach today, because I preached..." When I hung up the phone I realized that I never got to answer. It dawned on me that it had happened again. It was never about me, to begin with, and I missed it. Jesus wants us to fight that spirit and make one of our offerings to Him a meek spirit. I could assert myself in pursuit of my cause but I will instead humbly wait and make it about another person. What I do not get now I will inherit from Jesus.

This is perhaps one of the hardest spiritual disciplines to develop because it is so countercultural. Everything today is about aggression, ferocious pursuit, stepping on and over people, and getting things done no matter what. But the Lord is teaching that sometimes you have to have the capacity to follow the leading of the Spirit to let it happen in God's time. Sometimes you could change the narrative and switch the lens from them to you, but whatever you would say would not be as strong as letting it be about them. Don't forget that God promises that He has written for your benefit. You will get yours, and you will not have to assert yourself to get it. No fighting will be required, no press will be necessary, and no cost will you have to pay. You will instead inherit it.

Jesus is our best example of meekness. When arrested and having the power to create His release, watching Judas use his closeness for his cause, and being able to circumvent the plans for His death if He chose to, Jesus instead surrendered to it to accomplish God's ultimate will for human redemption. As a result, there was given to Jesus a name that is above every name, and at that name, every knee shall bow and tongue confess.

What are you trying to pursue for your cause? The Lord is inviting you to engage with meekness so you can inherit it rather than fighting so hard for it. Some stuff just does not need you attacking it like it is war, even if it feels like it. Some stuff you have to pleasantly and humbly wait on the Lord to shape to be yours by inheritance and not by engagement and conflict. A.W. Tozer said:

> **The meek man cares not at all who is greater than he, for he has long ago decided that the esteem of**

the world is not worth the effort. The rest Christ offers is the rest of meekness, the blessed relief which comes when we accept ourselves for what we are and cease to pretend. It will take some courage at first, but the needed grace will come as we learn that we are sharing in this new and easy yoke with the strong Son of God Himself.

Charles Swindoll images meekness as "strength under control." I love this definition. Charles Swindoll goes on to say, "Meekness describes a wild stallion who was tamed and taught to be ridden. That stallion still has all the strength it had when it was wild, but now it is strength under control. It is strength bottled up for the master's use."

In *The Message* version, Matthew 5:5 says,

You're blessed when you're content with just who you are—no more, no less. That's the moment you find yourselves proud owners of everything that can't be bought. (MSG).

QUESTIONS FOR THOUGHT

1. Do you feel that you are living a life of meekness–strength under control–during this time of hardship?

2. Are you fighting for something that the Lord wants to give you by inheritance instead?

3. Can you relate to the idea of constantly being emptied to be filled instead with the presence of God?

LET US PRAY

Lord, we are grateful for these moments. We are blessed to spend time meditating on You. Thank You for the rich deposits You make in our lives daily; we want to offer You passioned disciplines in return. Today, help us to accept the difficult pursuit of living meek lives: Carrying the power to change what we instead wait on You to change for us. Having the power of decision but waiting on the Spirit to lead and guide us. Knowing what to do to advance goals and yet waiting on Your release and permission. We do want to live fortunate lives—blessed lives—and we accept the disciplines that come with it. We are excited about the challenge and enthused about the growth.

Protect us today and keep us healthy and strong. Keep our minds clear and bless our endeavors. Make us instruments for Your glory and help us to bless others' lives by the offering we make of our own lives. We ask it in Jesus' name. Amen.

DAY 19 MEDITATION

HUNGERING AND THIRSTING FOR JESUS

Matthew 5:6 reads:

Blessed are those who hunger and thirst for righteousness, for they will be filled.

Most Bible scholars believe those who heard Jesus say this could have interpreted it in a couple of ways:

1. There was an expectation of Jesus that those who would follow Him, believing He would lead a rebellion and topple government structures, would hear this as a promise of satisfaction in the afterlife if they survived suffering and persecution in this life.

2. Jesus intended a certain moral goodness of those who would follow Him. Those who would

follow Jesus would need to seek after it with all of their hearts and as a result, a reward would be given to them for their pursuit. This interpretation is problematic because no amount of effort could declare us righteous. We are only declared righteous because of our faith in Jesus.

There is a third option. It is interpreted based upon how the expression is written, which is indurative present tense or progressive present. This means that the hungering and thirsting continues; it never stops. The hungering and thirsting increase in the very act of being satisfied. So daily the Lord forgives, feeds, blesses, and creates this desire to want to be forgiven, fed, and blessed again. What Jesus has promised is that the continuation of your hunger is always going to be met by His continuation of provision. What are we hungering and thirsting for? Jesus says, "righteousness!" The easiest way to think about pursuing righteousness: doing God's will from the heart or living with a heart to do God's will.

God's will is for you to enjoy a relationship with Him, reflected in devotional life, a steady saturation in His Word, a healthy and robust worship life, and the consistent extension of His person to others in acts of service, and with the great virtue of love.

God has promised that if you live desiring to do God's will from your heart, He will keep fulfilling that desire. At the same time, God will create within you a continual desire to keep doing His will. So, the more you live wanting to do God's will, the more you will want to do God's will, and God will keep satisfying your want no matter how much it increases.

So, the invitation for us when we hear this promise is this: how strong is your desire to do God's will? With that our working definition of righteousness, how righteous are you? I am not talking about righteousness as measured by perfection which we would never be successful at attaining. But, if righteousness is measured by the intensity of our will to do God's will, then how righteous are you?

How do you increase your will to do His will? By accepting that God's purpose in your life is to keep you hungry and thirsty to do more of His will. Now do not hear this as a frustrating cycle that has no fulfillment or joy. It should be understood by each of us that the Lord does not want you to have to settle, or as Paul said, to think that you have already attained it.

The blessing God brings to your daily grind is this: He has more filling to offer than you can present righteousness.

Day 19 Meditation: Hungering and Thirsting for Jesus

Every time you mature in the capacity as it relates to wanting to do His will, He creates additional hunger by satisfying where you are at the present level.

Today, I want to expand my want to do God's will. The expansion of my capacity to do God's will is measured by how much more I want to do His will.

If you have reached a certain level in life, then the real attainment is not the level you have reached but the hunger and thirst it creates in you to reach the next level. The stronger you become, mentally and physically, is a blessing in that it creates a stronger will in you to be even more mentally and physically strong.

Your life is spiritually wired this way: if you are actively engaged with the Holy Spirit residing in you, then you cannot settle no matter how healthy you are. You are hungry to push your will to do God's will forward. However mentally strong you are, you are hungry to push it forward. Whatever project you are completing makes you hungry to take on the next one with more to accomplish and to attain. Whatever debt you pay off makes you want to pay off more debt. However deeply you love makes you want to love more deeply. Jesus calls these types of behavior righteousness. It's what a satisfied, well-fed, refreshed will look like.

If you want to know how righteous you are, then stop measuring it by what you do not do or by how well you have perfected what you do. Righteousness in this context is never being satisfied with anything but the hunger created in you by what Jesus has already satisfied.

When the kings of the Bible did not do what was right in the sight of the Lord, the Remnant went to praying. God heard their cries and sent them more than a human agent to inspire hope; God sent a change of season. You may just be living in that change of season for your life, you'll know for certain if you are hungering for more and thirsting for more. Don't ignore it.

Embrace the unsettledness, explore the restlessness, and linger around the thoughts God is inspiring in you because the more you seek to do His will, the more He will make you want to seek to do His will.

Dietrich Bonhoeffer got it right when he said, "Not only do the followers of Jesus renounce their rights, they renounce their righteousness too. They get no praise for their achievements or sacrifices. They cannot have righteousness except by hungering and thirsting for it this applies equally to their righteousness and the righteousness of God on earth). Always they look forward to the future righteousness of God, but they cannot establish it for themselves. Those who follow Jesus grow hungry and thirsty on the way."

Live your life hungry and thirsty to do God's will. The way God will satisfy your will is to make you hungrier and thirstier to do His will. Oh, what satisfaction that is.

QUESTIONS FOR THOUGHT

1. Has your current season of life made you hungrier and thirstier for righteousness?

2. How would you define "righteousness" after reading today's meditation?

3. If righteousness is measured by the intensity of your will to do God's will, then how righteous are you?

LET US PRAY

Thank You, Lord, for knowing what we need. That does not surprise us since You made us and did so in Your likeness and according to Your image. We are inspired today to feel grateful and appreciative of all that You have already done in our lives, but we confess that in every way that You have met needs, made ways, and answered prayers. It has made us want to journey farther and express our want for You to meet other needs and to answer weightier prayers. Today, we acknowledge this hunger as a work of grace You have wrought in us. We do not consider ourselves to have attained and we count all things but loss that we might win the greater prize of eternal fellowship with You. Our will is to always be hungry and thirsty to do Your will.

Now I pray that You will help us to inspire all who are around us to hunger and thirst to do Your will as well. We can never bring to You without You satisfying us and creating in us a want for more: more love, more power, more grace, more opportunity, and more anointing. We pray today not that You feed us till we want no more, but feed us till we want nothing but more. In Jesus' name, we pray. Amen.

DAY 20 MEDITATION

THE IMPORTANCE OF SHOWING MERCY

Matthew 5:7 says, Blessed are the merciful, for they will be shown mercy.

In an earlier meditation, I suggested that you study Scripture by beginning with who the writer is writing to and how the original hearers would have heard what was being communicated to them. It is hard to interpret the meaning of a text without knowing the writer and the context of the original hearers. The absence of this information becomes a breeding ground for what all of us have become victims of, which is proof-texting. My mother used to tell me that the Bible said I was to clean my room. I never found that passage. When God is silent, so am I. When God speaks, so do I. I asked my mother what book of the Bible records "clean my room". She said to me, "It goes something like this: cleanliness is next to godliness"! I suggested that it was not in there and her words were: "Well, it's what one of those passages mean."

Let's start today's meditation with who Jesus was talking to and why.

Jesus preached to extremely persecuted people who believed they were loved by God, but their suffering was making them feel abandoned and rejected by Him. Sounds familiar to the way many people think today. Jesus preached in contrast to what was being promoted from the synagogue. One of His interpretive methods was to help persecuted people to think beyond this life and to the guaranteed promises to be delivered in eternity. Jesus said as part of His protracted sermon, "Blessed are the merciful, for they will be shown mercy." Jesus' suffering listeners would have internalized it this way: "Despite that your persecutors are treating you mercilessly, you in return show them mercy so that when God completes the ushering in and establishment of His kingdom on the Earth, God will treat you mercifully." The implication that they would have internalized after this ushering in of God's kingdom on the Earth, those merciless people will be treated by God without mercy.

I would suspect that this resonated with those who heard it. Take the struggle now and do not retaliate in a way that disqualifies you from receiving mercy spiritually, which is far more important to your life. I want to frame it in a way that makes it a better staging for our meditation time: You will live a happy, fortunate, and blessed life when you care, because offering care will result in you being cared for by God!

Let me expand it just a tad, like an eye doctor who flips those lenses from one to two and creates a little more clarity in your vision. Don't stop caring, including times when your care doesn't seem like an appropriate response to the way they are treating you. But do it anyway, because in extending care you are creating the capacity to receive it from God.

How you care for others is measured by your understanding of the larger things that are of value that are at stake in your life. Here is a theological principle that I don't want you to ever forget. It will extremely bless your life and make dealing with people so much easier. You are living your reality with split attachment all the time. Everything you say and do and the ways you interact with other people have to be on your mind both for how you extend out towards people but also how you extend in towards God. Both your relationship with others and your relationship with God can be impacted by the decisions you make on either side.

Jesus taught that the open hand of care you extend to others, including those who are being unworthy of the care you are providing, leaves that hand open to receive God's care, including the times you are taking the privilege of relationship with Him for granted. When you close that hand and refuse to care for others, that hand is closed when the Lord extends care to you. It will not be because God is merciless in response to your life but because your hands are closed and unable to receive from God.

Mercy is not sentiment. Mercy is an action that leads one to spare a person what they deserve or to extend help when they do not deserve it. Mercy is counter-cultural. It hits at first as weakness or passivity, but not when you consider that extending care is part of protecting your relationship with God. You need to keep the channel of blessing open.

This is what Jesus was getting at-you live in two spheres. To keep your relationship with the Lord healthy, you have to manage unhealthy human relationships. The motivation to manage unhealthy human relationships with care is because you do not want to respond to an unhealthy human relationship in a way that makes you mismanage your relationship with God. This is so liberating. It is that spiritual place to which you need to go before you respond to someone in a way that pleases your flesh.

I could say, do, respond, or ignore, how God is leading because I must keep a clear and uncluttered relationship exchange with Him.

If you were to ask me what I want you to feel convicted about today, then it is this: Don't lose your ability to care, to show mercy, to feel pity for another person in a way that leads you to act on another's behalf. Don't lose that, because it does far more to benefit you than it does to disadvantage you. The way we respond to and initiate exchange with difficult people, the way we respond to and initiate an exchange with co-workers, the way we respond to and initiate an exchange with people in culture, have to be stewarded with this verse in mind. You are living for far more than one heated exchange or chance to get even by refusing to help, speak, or open a door for someone. You and I are bigger than that in Christ. We know that we care for and extend mercy because we are thinking about the bigger picture. We know that we live needing God to respond to, initiate an exchange, open a door, give us another chance, and extend to our care.

Matthew 25:40-45 reads:

> King: "I tell you this: whenever you saw a brother or sister hungry or cold, whatever you did to the least of these, so you did to Me."

> At that He will turn to those on His left hand.

> King: "Get away from Me, you despised people whom My Father has cursed. Claim your inheritance—the pits of flaming hell where the devil and his minions suffer. For I was starving, and you left Me with no food. When I was dry and thirsty, you left Me to struggle with nothing to drink. When I was alone as a stranger, you turned away from Me. When I was pitifully naked, you left Me unclothed. When I was sick, you gave Me no care. When I was in prison, you did not comfort Me."

> Unrighteous: "Master, when did we see You hungry and thirsty? When did we see You friendless or homeless or excluded? When did we see You without clothes? When did we see You

sick or in jail? When did we see You in distress and fail to respond?"

King: "I tell you this: whenever you saw a brother hungry or cold, when you saw a sister weak and without friends, when you saw the least of these and ignored their suffering, so you ignored Me." (VCE).

I hope you see it. You cannot make people deal with you any other way than how they choose, but you can deal with them with the bigger spiritual picture at stake in your mind. If you have to extend mercy to someone who deserves fierce and swift judgment then you must keep in mind that the investment you are making is for your spiritual benefit because you want to protect your relationship with God.

A high school basketball player's mom passed away on the day of a game. Still, the player made it to the game. His coach invited him to sit on the bench but the player wanted to play. Since he arrived late, putting him in the game was a technical foul and the other team would shoot two free throws. Knowing the situation, the other team refused to shoot the free throws. But the officials persisted. The coach asked for a volunteer to shoot the shots and the captain raised his hand. His first shot went about two feet, his second went about one foot. The other team showed mercy to this player by sharing his pain with acts of kindness.

The grieving player may have set the team up to lose the game, but that whole team won a chance to mature their characters.

QUESTIONS FOR THOUGHT

1. Can you think of a time when you showed mercy instead of retaliating?

2. Can you think of a time you were shown mercy by someone else?

3. What has your current situation and circumstances taught you about mercy?

LET US PRAY

Lord, forgive us when we, at times, forget the larger things that are at stake with the decisions we make and the ways we respond to people. We admit that anger gets the best of us at times—the way people initiate an exchange with us or respond to us makes us less focused on our relationship with You and more focused on responding in what we believe is a demonstration of strength. Thank You for convicting us to always have in our spirits the larger picture of spiritual implication for the decisions we make and the reactions we offer to others.

You have indeed been so merciful to us and we know that we can extend mercy in response. Thank You that Your strength is in fact and in faith made perfect in our human weaknesses. We will wrestle the pull of our fleshly natures that want to render evil for evil, and instead, we will extend care and mercy lavishly on others out of gratitude for the care and mercy You so lavishly pour on our lives. Strengthen us with this lesson in mind. In Jesus' name, we pray. Amen.

DAY 21 MEDITATION

JOURNALING YOUR JOURNEY

Today, spend time in prayer and reflection on what you have digested in this week's meditations. Record your thoughts, emotions, insights, and prayers on the following pages. "Journaling your journey" through this difficult time in your life not only serves to help you process your experience at the moment but will be something you can look back on in the future as evidence of how God has worked in your life.

_____

_____

_____

_____

Day 21 Meditation: Journaling Your Journey

_____

_____

_____

_____

_____

_____

_____

_____

_____

_____

_____

Day 21 Meditation: Journaling Your Journey

_____

_____

_____

_____

_____

_____

_____

_____

_____

_____

DAY 22 MEDITATION

HAPPY IS THE PURE AT HEART

Today we read Matthew 5:8, which says, "Blessed are the pure in heart, for they will see God."

There are two ways to interpret this verse. Some believe it to mean "inner moral purity" as opposed to external piety. This leans on passages like Psalm 24:3-6:

> Who may ascend the mountain of the Lord?
>
> Who may stand in his holy place?
>
> The one who has clean hands and a pure heart,
>
> who does not trust in an idol
>
> or swear by a false god.
>
> They will receive blessing from the Lord

and vindication from God their Savior.

Such is the generation of those who seek him,

who seek your face, God of Jacob.

The emphasis is not on the physical ascent or the intentional entrance into the Holy Place but on the inner condition of the one who desires to enter. So, one way of interpreting what Jesus meant when He said "pure of heart" may have been with this in mind.

The other way that some have interpreted this verse is that it is suggesting "singlemindedness."

Theologically, this means to be "free from the tyranny of a divided self". We are not to live as a hypocrite, which means to move around as if wearing a mask, acting out in whatever character necessary to protect self-interest, to support the values of a system, or to be loyal to those in whose circle it is important for one to belong.

I wrestle with having to choose sides on this issue. There is value in seeing pure in heart with singlemindedness as synergy and not separate. If a person is single-minded in their pursuit to live with a commitment to the kingdom of God, then He will not let you be inwardly contaminated. If you are surrendering to Jesus to make you inwardly clean, then it is hard for you to play-act your way through systems, whether it be the job, your circle of relationships, or as a citizen in this country.

Francis and Clare of Assisi lived their lives in search of both inner and outer freedom, or what Jesus says is to live "pure in heart." Francis and Clare found a radical way to do this. I am not suggesting it, but I want to describe it, so we can borrow a description of it for our spiritual discipline.

Francis and Clare's agenda for justice was radical and protest-driven. They did not seek to find a comfortable compromise with evil systems, nor did they demand that the system do right through policy and legislation. They instead felt led to shape lifestyles outside of the system. For them, that meant taking a vow of poverty. It also meant a conscious decision to commune with people pushed to the outer edges of life. What Francis and Clare found was not activity around peace and justice. They became peace and justice in lifestyle. The descriptor that was attached to their lives is that it invites us to modify our own lives in this season. They learned to "live on the edge of the inside."

Jesus meant, "a happy person is one that has a pure heart." People cannot be co-opted because they feel like the job supports the oversized house they live in and the luxury car they drive. People can speak their convictions because they are not so attached to any relationship until they cannot appreciate its season. People do not have to be silent about the evil in a system because they are dependent on that system for security and a sense of belonging.

Jesus wants us to surrender to Him to shape us with inner authenticity based on our being followers of Him and then to also find our place on the edge of the inside. That is living so in your spiritual reality that you never become too vulnerable to be crushed by this natural reality we live in, which is nothing more than a web of varied systems that Jesus called the world.

Don't be in any relationship where you have to suppress who you are and what you believe to make another feel important or empowered when to do so means sacrificing yourself. Now, I understand that there are times when we all have to tame the tongue and say what is wise rather than what is raw—to choose when to say something rather than being irresponsible with timing and sacrificing content. But

I want you to hear me when I say, you need to steward your life to be able to live on the inside of the edge.

Manage your money in such a way that you are not a prisoner to the job you work on. Develop authentic relationships where you do not have to be somebody else for them because it is so important for you to be attached. Be able to celebrate as much when it demands separating from things, experiences, or people as you do when they are first connected to you.

You can only develop this kind of purity of heart when you trust that God was providential with how He shaped your "authentic" self. Since God was free to be creatively imaginative, it also means He was purposely intentional with every detail about you. You cannot sacrifice any of it to belong, or to finance something that makes it look like you belong. Find your place on the inside of the edge. Remember that we traffic in this world, but we are not of this world. We are born from above. We walk this temporal plain in pursuit of a heavenly dwelling that is eternal.

I am not minimizing anything that I have taught in past meditations, but this for me ranks high, because it determines how you build your life from budgeting your future to choosing where you will work, to what you will buy, to how you use the phrase "I need that." It includes who you will vote for and what will be your emotional health as you grieve the loss of things and what will be your level of excitement when the season demands certain attachments for your life.

Happy is the one that has found in his or her heart that place inside the edge where they have learned to protect who they are in the kingdom of God and never want that co-opted by systems or people.

If the heart is the seat of the emotions, then Jesus is teaching that the seat of your emotions cannot be mixed because you are only partially loyal to the kingdom and at the same time wearing the mask in the public square. If that is the description of your life, then the prayer is that God would start ordering everything in your life in such a way that you are left standing on the inside of the edge– ready to move when the Spirit nudges, courageous to say what needs to be said, excited to learn and humble enough to be corrected, speaking the truth in power to systems of oppression, owning nothing you cannot let go of if necessary, and fully recognizing that seasons change and sometimes with the changing so do the patterns of certain relationships.

This is what Jesus means when he says, "Blessed are the pure in heart." Let's not forget the promise: "They will see God"! Remember this is being spoken to persecuted people who are suffering in time. One of the ways we interpret this is "they will see God" in eternity as a reward for managing the inside of the edge faithfully.

But the second way of understanding this is to think of the words "confirmation" and "discernment". When you live free enough, as Paul says, to "be content" when abounding or in need, when you can say what you feel convicted to say and perhaps have to pay in ways that will be inconvenient, and yet be okay, then you are moving in the direction of a pure heart. When it matters more that you are led by Jesus than accepted by a person or persons, then you are headed in the direction of a pure heart. When you can risk losing what is of great value for you to protect who you are, then you are on your way to a pure heart.

God promises that while walking the path to a pure heart, He will let you see Him in confirmations and discernments that affirm that you are indeed headed in the right direction.

I love how author Mark Hart puts it because to me it describes this "inside of the edge" image I am trying to seed-plant in you. He says:

To love someone properly probably means that you won't be very popular. Pure love, loving the way it was intended, is unfortunately a foreign concept to many. Love is messy. Love will involve hardship, demand patience, require forgiveness, test maturity, strain friendship, challenge priorities, refine character, ignite the heart, and unleash the soul. Love is not something you sing about; it's the reason you sing. Love is not something you write about; it's the reason you write. Love is not something you live to find; it's the reason that you are alive.

QUESTIONS FOR THOUGHT

1. Which of the above-mentioned explanations of being "pure in heart" do you tend toward? Why?

2. In your own words, how would you describe living "inside of the edge"?

3. Has your current time of growth, suffering, and difficulty allowed you to see God in new ways?

LET US PRAY

Lord, we confess that this challenge You have laid out before us is so inviting because it rings loud bells of inner freedom and genuine authenticity. It does free our minds to imagine without the pull of attachments and loyalties, which pull with such strength in other directions. My prayer is that wherever we are inside Your kingdom today, we would use that powerful place to move more to the inside of the edge of this world. Help us to be less dependent on this world for our personhood, our livelihood, and our hope for the future. We gladly announce that our hope is built on nothing less than Jesus' blood and His righteousness. We pray in Jesus' name. Amen.

DAY 23 MEDITATION

BLESSED ARE THE PEACEMAKERS

Matthew 5:9 reads:

Blessed are the peacemakers, for they will be called children of God.

Let's first consider how these words were heard by those to whom they were originally written: "Happy are those who love peace". More specifically, it means to fight to make sure that all parts are joined together. Happy are those who fight and work hard to make sure that people who live at variance find a way to eliminate it. Of course, the variance is eliminated by helping opposing sides to surrender to the common redemption we share in Christ. In Him, we are not as far apart on anything as we think we are. Salvation is needed by everyone. Grace is available to everyone. Everyone sees through a glass darkly. Everyone is prone to make mistakes. Everyone needs a chance to outlive mistakes and failures in judgment.

"Peacemaker" probably should read "peace-worker" because it implies a person who sees variance and seeks to eliminate it. As you might see, the key is we are invited to chase happiness not by being peace-hopers but peacemakers—to use our capacity, to steward our space, to initiate our relationship engagements with this in mind.

God wants to use you to stand in the middle of variance between people whose disagreements might be sharp. God wants you to work your gifts, your discernment, and the empowerment that comes with a relationship with the Holy Spirit, which gives you access to the supernatural. We are so saturated with what promotes disagreement that we forget that as Christians we are implored spiritually to fight to find a place of agreement, a place of reconciliation, to see the hope and potential in the people around us, to see Peter not for what He will do to deny Christ but for how many he will strengthen after growing from that terrible moment.

Here's an illustration of peacemaking work:

Mr. Smith and Mr. Jones were "on the outs" over a trivial matter. This deeply concerned Deacon Brown, so he prayed that he might be a peacemaker. He called on Smith and asked, "What do you think of Jones?"

"He's the meanest crank in the neighborhood!"

"But," said Brown, "you have to admit that he's very kind to his family."

The next day Deacon Brown went to Jones and inquired, "Do you know what Smith said about you?"

"No, but I can imagine how that scamp would lie about me!"

"This may surprise you, but he said you're very kind to your family."

"What! Did Smith say that?"

"Yes, he did."

"Well, if you hadn't told me, I wouldn't believe it."

"What do you think of Smith?" asked Deacon Brown.

"Truthfully, I believe he's a lowdown scalawag,

but you have to admit that he's very honest in business."

"Yes, there's no getting around that; in business he's a man you can trust."

The next day deacon Brown called on Smith again. "You know what Jones said about you? He claims you're a fellow that really can be trusted in business, and that you're scrupulously honest."

"You mean it?"

"Yes, I do," said Brown.

"Well, of all things," replied Smith with a happy smile.

The next Sunday the former "enemies" nodded to each other. Deacon Brown continued his "meddling" until the next annual business meeting of the church when Smith and Jones shook hands and finally voted on the same side!

So the question is, "where is God trying to use you to be a peacemaker?" Peacemaking is ministry. Peacemaking is the offering we give to God, but I want to stress it is work.

There was a young soldier boy who was a Christian. After the lights were out in the barracks, he would slip down on his knees by his bunk to pray. One night the sergeant, who had little use for anything religious or Christian, threw his muddy boots at the boy, striking him on the side of the head.

The next morning, the sergeant found his boots beside his bed all clean and polished to perfection. The sergeant was so impressed by the actions of the young man that he was eventually reached for the Lord. The sergeant accepted salvation. "Blessed are the peacemakers, for they will be called sons of God."

James 3:17 tells us:

> **But the wisdom that comes from Heaven is first of all pure; then peace-loving, considerate, submissive, full of mercy and good fruit, impartial and sincere. Peacemakers who sow in peace reap a harvest of righteousness.**

- Dr. Martin Luther King said, "When we look at modern man, we have to face the fact...that modern man suffers from a kind of poverty of the spirit, which stands in glaring contrast to his scientific and technological abundance; we've learned to fly the air like birds, we've learned to swim the seas like fish, and yet we haven't learned to walk the earth as brothers and sisters..."

- Nelson Mandela said, "The first thing is to be honest with yourself. You can never have an impact on society if you have not changed yourself...Great peacemakers are all people of integrity, of honesty, but humility."

- Maya Angelou said, "If you are always trying to be normal, you will never know how amazing you can be."

"Blessed are the peacemakers"—they will be called children of God.

Jesus died on a cross and was resurrected for the sins of humanity to make the ultimate peace.

QUESTIONS FOR THOUGHT

1. Is there a peacemaker that you know personally, or that you know of, whom you would like to emulate?

2. Why is peacemaking such difficult work?

3. Can you think of parties in your life who could use your peacemaking efforts?

LET US PRAY

Lord, our prayer today is that You would make us peacemakers who are unafraid to stand in the middle of the human divide and work to create reconciling moments where You might bless us with Your presence, bringing us peace that surpasses all human understanding. We will put our hands to the plow and refuse to look back. Thank You for calming the raging tides inside of us and giving us peace so that we might extend it to others in Your name.

Day 23 Meditation: Blessed are the Peacemakers

Thank You that of all You do in our lives, You also make us peacemakers. I pray this virtue will fill every one of us and that we honor You in the places where we have relationships for Your glory and the expansion of Your kingdom on the Earth. In Jesus' name, we pray. Amen.

DAY 24 MEDITATION

SUFFERING FOR CHRIST

The first four Beatitudes emphasize the persecuted condition of those who are disciples of Jesus. Poor in spirit, mourning, meek, and hungering and thirsting for righteousness: these describe the conditions disciples lived in during times of persecution. However, the last four Beatitudes emphasize the ethical qualities you would expect to see characterized in disciples even during times of persecution. They are to be merciful, pure in heart, peacemakers, and righteous, which in this portion of Scripture is defined by what is acceptable behavior to God.

Jesus' teaching suggests that persecution creating these tough conditions would normally not result in these behaviors unless there was the presence and influence of the Lord in one's life. Being a Christian and desiring to be faithful as a disciple informs how you think, how you process life, how you interact with others and is manifested in biblically defined behavior. These behaviors are counter-cultural and in many ways are unnatural to us.

The presence of Jesus does not guarantee exemption from the things that try men's souls, but His presence ought to change how we walk through them. Afflictions cannot sanctify a person, except as they are used by God to this end. There are times when the Lord uses affliction to sanctify us, and then there are times that the Lord allows affliction to prove how yielded we are to Him. This is both for our observation and to evangelize others.

Jesus began to round out His teaching with verse 10 of Matthew 5: "Blessed are those who are persecuted because of righteousness, for theirs is the kingdom of heaven."

Let's illuminate it slightly with the Amplified interpretation: "Blessed [comforted by inner peace and God's love] are those who are persecuted for doing that which is morally right, for theirs is the kingdom of Heaven [both now and forever]".

The word "persecuted" in the Greek means to be chased. It is the image of someone chasing you down as if hunting an animal. You are pursued because you live morally in pursuit of what is acceptable to God. You are treated a certain way because you live by faith in Jesus Christ. When you fight to live, chasing what is morally acceptable to God, you will suffer for it. This is what Jesus taught. In addition, Jesus' teachings are always constructing bridges with Old Testament teaching, because it was never the Lord's intent to destroy law with the gospel, but to fulfill it. Given this bridge, Jesus was always connecting. This verse is connected to Psalm 15:1-2, which says:

> **Lord, who may dwell in your sacred tent?**
>
> **Who may live on your holy mountain?**
>
> **The one whose walk is blameless,**
>
> **who does what is righteous,**
>
> **who speaks the truth from their heart.**

The Psalm describes righteousness. It also has echoes from the prophet Isaiah:

Day 24 Meditation: Suffering for Christ

Hear me, you who know what is right,

you people who have taken my instruction to heart:

Do not fear the reproach of mere mortals

or be terrified by their insults. Isaiah 51:7

The passage deals with the persecution. The message is clear: if you are a Christian who has matured to shaping your ethic around what is pleasing to God, then you will be pursued by people who, like those hunting animals, will create stress, discomfort, and threat in your life. The question is not concerning the reality of this teaching point Jesus is making. The question is: knowing I will be persecuted for following Jesus, what is my life's response?

I want to suggest that persecution is not just physically extended by people, but it can also be the words they have planted that have caused internal, head-and-heart issues. You may be chased and pursued by that one comment that has you doubting yourself or a severe threat that has you cautious to dream big and to aim high. It may be the images people have created that let you know that your color and your kind are tolerated but not appreciated. I tend to believe that we live more under the pressure of internal persecution.

Jesus says to those being persecuted that if they live morally acceptable to Him, then in the end they will be rewarded with the kingdom.

How do I live every day in pockets and places under the pressure of persecution? How do I fight the internal battle of being persecuted by thoughts and emotions and the remembrance of experiences that are chasing me in my head and heart every day? Here is the answer: you decide that part of being a disciple is not just how you receive from the Lord blessings, answered prayers, provisions, and protection, but part of being a disciple is in how you contend for the faith. We want to approach our week prayerfully, peacefully, productive, safe, and stress-free. The Lord can provide each of these traits to our approach to prayer. However, for some of us in some of our spaces and some of our encounters, we will have to contend for the faith. You will have to fight for it. The one-chapter book of Jude says this in verse 3:

Beloved, while I was very diligent to write to you concerning our common salvation, I found it necessary to write to you exhorting you to contend earnestly for the faith which was once for all delivered to the saints. (NKJV).

Contend for your faith. This means give particular focus on the fact that you will have to compete against things that are trying to make you abandon your faith. I do not mean "abandon" in the sense of walking away from Jesus, but I suggest "abandon" in terms of decisions, reactions, absorptions, considerations, conversations, and confrontations. Jude uses the word "contend" intentionally because it means you skillfully commit to competing.

You already know in what areas the enemy is coming after you this week, so pray about those areas and read Scripture that speaks to the issues that you will face in those areas. Ask God to let the Spirit prepare that place or interaction. Call people who flank you in prayer, ask them to long-range position themselves on the hill and provide your prayer sniper cover for the unseen attacks planned for you. Then, as you are fighting the fight, they are taking care of your peripheral issues.

What kind of week do you want? No matter how you answer that question, I want you to apply this theme this week "Contending for the faith." Say these things to yourself: "Yes, I am waiting on God. Yes, I am believing God. Yes, I am anticipating. But I am going to do another thing this week: I am going to compete for the kind of week I vision for my life. I will fight for it, and I will fight with skill. Since I have skill in this fight I will fight with the true weapon of my warfare, which is not carnal but spiritual."

The weapons we fight with are not the weapons of the world. On the contrary, they have divine power to demolish strongholds. (II Corinthians 1:4).

I know it is hard to believe that you have to fight to live your life according to God's will. But the prince of the air, the enemy, is always trying to squeeze your life and stress it to the point where you will surrender to thinking, emoting, and then reacting in ways that will be contrary to what is acceptable behavior for a disciple of Jesus. R.C. Sproul says this: "Defending the faith to the best of our ability is not a luxury or an indulgence in intellectual vanity. It is the task given to each one of us as we bear witness to our faith before the world."

QUESTIONS FOR THOUGHT

1. Do you believe that the Lord can use your current affliction to sanctify you and to test your faith?

2. Can you view your current struggle not as a place for punishment, but as an arena to contend for your faith?

3. What are some ways you can prepare for the battles that await you today and this week?

LET US PRAY

Lord, I pray this week that as much as we are waiting on You and depending on, You for our well-being and the shaping of our days, we also become convicted about our need to fight for the prioritized placement of our faith in our daily exchanges. May we never forget that we are being persecuted in so many ways for our righteousness, and rather than be deflated about this or drained by it, I pray You release in us the will to want to fight.

You have brought us too far for us to give up now. We will pull down every persecuting thought and imagination that attempts to exalt itself above the knowledge of Christ. We choose to walk this week sober-minded and spiritually resolute that we are engaged in a battle. We intend to win it for the cause of Christ. Lift our emotions and help us to accept where You have planted us, the weapons You have given us, and the battle that is before us. We already know that the victory is ours. To that end, grant us grace to fight for the peace You promised us, to fight for the blessings You have bestowed upon us, to fight for the grace You have released into our lives.

May we remember our need to contend in every conversation and every counter thought. Thank You that You have made us mighty in You. Strengthen us by Your Word. May we be encouraged by the flanked support we receive from the body. In all of this, we ask for Your glory and the expansion of Your kingdom here on Earth, in Jesus' name. Amen.

DAY 25 MEDITATION

DEVELOPING ABSURD FAITH

One of my favorite thinkers is the Danish theologian Søren Kierkegaard. He said, "To dare is to lose one's footing momentarily. Not to dare is to lose oneself." I need you to dare today to hear these words from Jesus:

> **Blessed are you when people insult you, persecute you and falsely say all kinds of evil against you because of me. Rejoice and be glad, because great is your reward in heaven, for in the same way, they persecuted the prophets who were before you. (Matthew 5:11).**

I want to call this an "absurd faith". Absurd faith is having confidence in God to live in ways that appear unreasonable. Absurd faith is taking an only son and going to a mountain fully persuaded that it is wise to obey God, even if it means sacrificing your son because you trust the character of God. Abraham trusted that God had to have a plan beyond Isaac's death. Absurd faith is to build an ark in a drought and anticipation of rain simply because you feel God's push for you to do it. Absurd faith is to stand in front of the king like Peter and teach about Jesus, knowing it may result in your execution. Absurd faith is having confidence in God to live in ways that appear unreasonable.

It is unreasonable to think that I would be expected to rejoice with people's insults, persecutions, vilifying my name, and spreading lies about me. I find it easier to believe that my faith can move mountains than to consider that my faith can help me to respond to people's mistreatment—the likes of which Jesus describes in this verse—and match it with rejoicing. Read the verse in *The Message* translation. While it is still absurd, it has a hint of encouragement for us:

Not only that—count yourselves blessed every time people put you down or throw you out or speak lies about you to discredit me. What it means is that the truth is too close for comfort and they are uncomfortable. You can be glad when that happens—give a cheer, even!—for though they

don't like it, I do! And all heaven applauds. And know that you are in good company. My prophets and witnesses have always gotten into this kind of trouble.

How do we do this? I know you will catch the lesson after reading this illustration:

A boy asked his father, "Dad, what is the size of God? How big is He?" The Father looked up at the sky and saw a little plane in the far distance and asked his son, "What is the size of the plane in the sky?" The boy replied, "It is really small. I can hardly see it in the sky." Then, the father said, "Son, let's go on a trip to the airport. I want to show you something." The boy jumped in his father's truck and off they went to the airport.

As they approached the plane, the father asked his son: "Now, son, how big is this plane?" The boy looked at the airplane and said, "Wow, Dad, that plane is huge! It's a lot bigger than that plane in the sky, isn't it!"

Then the father put his arm around his son and said, "Son, God's size is like this plane. It is the same one you saw in the sky from a distance and

it looked so small. God's size depends on how close or how far you are to Him. The closer you are, the bigger God looks!"

You cannot begin to offer God this kind of response to human cruelty and mistreatment unless you inch your life closer to Him. His big-sized goodness can affect your life in ways that shape a radically different perspective for you—where it is more important that God be pleased with you and you endure the repercussions of that from people who will aggravate your life because of it.

Dr. King said, "The early Christians rejoiced when they were deemed worthy to suffer for what they believed. In those days, the Church was not merely a thermometer that recorded the ideas and principles of popular opinion; it was a thermostat that transformed the mores of society."

We are being invited—some might consider it a challenge and others an invitation—to carry a heavyweight. Nonetheless, Jesus is inviting us to live with an absurd faith—to live beyond reason and to trust Him in a realm only occupied by those who have been transformed by the renewal of their minds. Hear it one more time and then I will give you some things to consider:

How ecstatic you can be when people insult and persecute you and speak all kinds of cruel lies about you because of your love for me! So leap for joy—since your heavenly reward is great. For you are being rejected the same way the prophets were before you.

Rejoice—why? Because apparently, your attempts to imitate Jesus have been successful. If following Jesus in faith means for you that you attempt to live your life as He lived and to treat people as He did and people are taking their persecution to this level because of His presence in your life, then that must mean you are doing extremely well at imitating Jesus. Rejoice over that. It is a confirmation of sorts. It says that you are reflecting His presence in ways that make it hard for people to interpret anything other than that you have been with Jesus.

Rejoice—why? Because it is a token of His grace. That is what Bonhoeffer calls it. He said: "Discipleship means allegiance to the suffering Christ and it is therefore not at all surprising that Christians should be called upon to suffer. It is a joy and a token of His grace....In the hour of the cruelest torture [martyrs] bear for His sake, they are made partakers in the perfect joy and bliss of fellowship with Him."

Rejoice—why? Because it invites you into the center of a functional Christology. By Christology, we mean the study of the nature of Christ, of which there are essentially two camps. A high Christology starts with Jesus' divinity and a low Christology starts with Jesus' humanity. My theology is informed by a high Christology, but my devotional life is enriched more by a low Christology—so neither is more right or wrong than the other. When I think of Christ seeking understanding of my faith from looking at the airplane on the ground, God is majestic. The words that come to mind are huge, massive, intimidating, and awe-inspiring. When I am exercising my devotions, nurturing my spiritual growth, and maturity I think of Jesus as a friend that sticks closer than a brother—a friend whom I can talk to about anything at any time on any level using whatever words best reflect my authentic emotions.

When I read about what was said about Him cruelly, what was done to Him in towns and villages where He was met with rejection, attempts to stone Him, trap Him, tempting Him, I feel closer to Him. When I read about Him weeping over a friend's death, angry over temple practices that exploited the least of these hear Him rebuke Peter and correct the disciples, I feel such a sense of closeness that it makes what people do to be less painful. Then His command to rejoice is doable because it confirms how close we have been to Him. It reminds me that He is acquainted with my grief and understands my sorrow.

Rejoice, because God gives you the ability to find the joy in it! I think of my relationship with Jesus as benefiting me in so many ways. One of them is the difference in the perspective I gain by knowing Him. I see things differently and think about them with divine purposes in mind. I emote things differently, considering the spiritual intention of things and not just the temporal or natural embrace of things.

> **We all know people who have been made much meaner and more irritable and more intolerable to live with by suffering: it is not right to say that all suffering perfects. It only perfects one type of person—the one who accepts the call of God in Christ Jesus. Oswald Chambers.**

I do not think you can fully show up to anything or endure anything until you can find the joy in it. What we go through is bearable because of the joy we get out of honoring the Lord through it. It is absurd to think that there is any joy in being treated like Jesus describes until you realize how much God trusts you to own Him and to grab your sense of delight when faced with what would make most people give up and curse Him.

One anonymous writer said: "I rejoice in life for its own sake. Life is no brief candle for me. It's a sort of splendid torch which I've got hold of for the moment, and I want to make it burn as brightly as possible before handing it on to future generations."

You are happy when people act and talk in a bad way to you and make it very hard for you and tell bad things and lies about you because you trust in Me. Be glad and full of joy because your reward will be much in heaven. They made it very hard for the early preachers who lived a long time before you. (NLV).

QUESTIONS FOR THOUGHT

1. Why can the faith you believe in be considered an "absurd faith"?

2. Does your current time of difficulty include a level of persecution? In drawing closer to Jesus through your suffering, do you think that it potentially could?

3. If, in suffering and persecution, you can be made more like Jesus, then does that change your perspective of it?

LET US PRAY

Lord, help us to live with this kind of perspective that Jesus teaches about. To endure the encounters in life that are intended for our harm in such a way that we can rejoice about them for the sheer privilege of being compared to Your great presence in creation.

We will gladly bear the struggle, endure the suffering in Your name, and thank You that You have promised to reward us with the kingdom. Wherever we are privileged to be in Your presence is the place of our greatest desire. We do not say it much, but for all that You endured for our redemption and to secure our eternal abode, we can handle living with lies, persecution, and all that goes along with it.

Today, we choose to rejoice, and we are honored to be associated with You, to be described by Your name and Your person, and to be treated in any way because of You. You have never disowned us, and we will not, now or in the future, disown You. In Jesus' name, we pray. Amen.

DAY 26 MEDITATION

STEWARDING YOUR AWAKENING

I can always tell when God is calling me to accept a fresh "awakening." By that, I mean a lifting or raising in my self-awareness, my understanding of God, and His progressive will for me. Some might call it discernment, which is probably accurate. I would suggest that discernment deals with distinguishing spirits, but awakening is different. Awakening is seeing everything around you differently while it is yet the same. It is hearing the same sounds but they are saying something different. Awakening is emoting things differently for the first time and being lifted in consciousness that this different feeling means something spiritual and is inviting you to interpret differently or reinterpret properly. I always know when I am being invited by God to awaken to a different "next season" with Him and for me.

I can tell people are talking but it is like God hit the mute button and I am hearing His words instead—like they are being downloaded during a software upgrade. I am engaged in the same interactions, but it is making me think about life on a whole different level. It is best described as what happens to us all when we tell people "I heard you say that before, but it hit me differently this time."

It is best reflected in terms of social commentary in the fact that for reasons that may be only God knows, the death of George Floyd sparked an "awakening" that is different. We had too many deaths to not already feel angry, frustrated, fatigued, and passionate. Rodney King's beating was as heart-wrenching as the knee on George Floyd's neck, but we see them differently. It is as if, for some, scales have been removed, headphones are taken off, and from this lifted awakening place, they see with new eyes and hear with new ears. Romans 13:11 says this:

> **Do this, knowing that this is a critical time. It is already the hour for you to awaken from your sleep [of spiritual complacency]; for our salvation is nearer to us now than when we first believed [in Christ]. (AMP).**

In Romans 13, Paul is teaching the Christian's obligation to see government theologically. That is, to understand that God permits it for cultural structure. It is as if Paul were being asked "What is our faith posture when it comes to the government while living as followers of Christ?" When Paul gets to verse 11, he transitions. Paul is then lifting the urgency to love and walk right with God because our salvation, he says, is closer than it has ever been.

The dominant words Paul used were "stay awake"! It is lifting, raising, and stirring. It does not happen once or twice. We are invited to these "awakening seasons" over and over again to the degree that we do not get stuck in any one season. You and I are at a critical hour where we are being invited to surrender to the Lord to lift us to a "higher spiritual awakening."

If God began major shifts in your life, then how would you know it? How would you feel about what you have grown so comfortable with? How excited would you be to be introduced to the better version of yourself? What would you mourn knowing part of you must remain behind? These are the questions that swirl in your head and heart when the God-initiated lift has reached the critical start stage.

Dr. King in the last sermon he preached before he was assassinated urged us to "remain awake through a great revolution." The worst thing we can do is to sleep through an awakening moment. God never intends for you to spiritually plateau, to settle in space, place, or thought, because in every God-appointed "due season," we are being invited by Him to reach up to the lifted place where He wants us to reside for a while. The lifted place where the thinking demands deeper reflections, choices have weightier consequences, tasks pull on a different set of skills and gifts, and what you are playing, for now, has higher stakes.

I do not care how old or young you are, how credentialed or not, every one of us is entering a new sphere of self-awareness.

Once God lifts you, you cannot do life the same. You will not hear people the same as you did before. It will appear as if God's voice has gotten louder and that you are now unsettled because the slingshot and harp have to be replaced with the scepter and the crown. Returning to fishing after seeing Jesus resurrected is like putting your hand to the plow and looking back. Your awareness of His resurrection is for the ministry ahead, not the ministry behind.

Dr. Barbara Holmes says that awakening or awareness is the moment when we rise with eyes crusted from self-induced dreams of what is control, domination, victimization, and hatred—catch a glimpse of the divine in the face of the other. There we are greeted with "I am that I am" and "I will be who I will be." It becomes a liberating example of awareness, mutuality, and self-revelation.

Awareness for you is not the confidence with which you say, "I am who I am." Awareness is the courage to admit that "I will be who I will be." In between these two includes periodic awakenings that the Lord uses to reveal that you are not yet your best self and pushes the needle towards it.

I am a rescuer by nature. I listen to problems, not for empathy, and to simply be compassionate. I listen for how I can solve it, fix it, eliminate it, or resource it. In many ways, my rescuer nature has served me well at a critical season of "progressive awakening" God challenged me about my "why" for living the way I do. Part of it was a germinating seed of a "God complex" where you think you can fix anything or that you are the last resort. The purging of that thought was to learn the value of the word "no." I remember how uncomfortable it was to say it early on. "I wish I could make that phone call for you or open that door for you or resource your dream, but I am not led to do that, but I will pray for you."

I did not know then what I know now that self-awareness inflection points are needed for decisions in front of me. I could not fix any of these issues– only God can. That is my way of saying God had to take me through awakenings so that I would be able to respond differently now.

Let's say that you are being ushered into an "awakening season." How do you steward this?

- Let the bush burning but not being consumed pull on your curiosity. Moses could have ignored the burning bush and with it being strange could have been all the more reason why he should have ignored it. But he treated it as an invitation. When these kinds of things are happening around you that are grabbing your attention in ways you had not noticed before, then go with it and explore it.

- Accept that as a child of God, your norm is to be comfortable with being uncomfortable. Faith is never totally settled because what makes it faith is its' need to seek, search, question, speculate, ask, and pray. When you stop doing these things, it is closely akin to walking by sight. Don't ever become so comfortable with being comfortable in control and relying on the calculated that you cannot be awakened to another level where everything about you will have to experience a shift to handle the assignment God has for you.

- Know the price that sleepwalking demands. When you sleepwalk through life, you have to pay with the currency of forfeiture. What you lose might be a divinely intended future. Because some of God's plans are specific to seasons, to not take advantage of them in a particular season is to perhaps lose them forever. So stay awake, because falling asleep costs too much.

Let's read Matthew 26:36-46.

Then Jesus went with his disciples to a place called Gethsemane, and he said to them, "Sit here while I go over there and pray." He took Peter and the two sons of Zebedee along with him, and he began to be sorrowful and troubled. Then he said to them, "My soul is overwhelmed with sorrow to the point of death. Stay here and keep watch with me."

Going a little farther, he fell with his face to the ground and prayed, "My Father, if it is possible, may this cup be taken from me. Yet not as I will, but as you will."

Then he returned to his disciples and found them sleeping. "Couldn't you men keep watch with me for one hour?" he asked Peter. "Watch and pray so that you will not fall into temptation. The spirit is willing, but the flesh is weak."

He went away a second time and prayed, "My Father, if it is not possible for this cup to be taken away unless I drink it, may your will be done."

When he came back, he again found them sleeping, because their eyes were heavy. So he left them and went away once more and prayed the third time, saying the same thing.

Then he returned to the disciples and said to them, "Are you still sleeping and resting? Look, the hour has come, and the Son of Man is delivered into the hands of sinners. Rise! Let us go! Here comes my betrayer!"

Accept that you are walking into an awakening season. You do not want to miss it.

QUESTIONS FOR THOUGHT

1. In what ways are your circumstances and trials awakening you from sleep?

2. Can you envision a time when you were comfortable with being uncomfortable?

3. Is it your natural tendency to want to fix, solve, and rescue things?

LET US PRAY

Lord, thank You that You do not ever let our faith become static. You have given us so great a salvation. We are so grateful for it. Our prayer is that we do not sleep through seasons in which You are sparking our next "awakenings." We do not want to miss Your will or sleep through our chance to put our hands to plow as demanded by this season. We will keep our lamps trimmed, burning, our discernment sharp, and spiritually connected. We are watching as well as praying and fighting to keep ourselves consecrated—all the things You require to ensure that we approach You with clean hands and pure hearts.

Day 26 Meditation: Stewarding Your Awakening

Where we have perhaps fallen asleep or are drifting into slumber, wake us up so we do not miss one second of Your intended plans and purposes in our lives. We ask it in Jesus' name. Amen

DAY 27 MEDITATION

THE IMPORTANCE OF A SPIRITUAL SECOND WIND

William James, the famed American philosopher, and psychologist said, "Most people never run far enough on their first wind to find out that they have a second wind."

Luke chapter 18 is Jesus' teaching on prayer and humility. In verse 1, Luke opened like a coach telling his or her players that they must push through to find their second wind.

Then Jesus told His disciples a parable to show them that they should always pray and not give up. The initial lesson in this teaching is about trusting that you have "second wind" capability in you. Life will force us to push past our threshold and find a way to function through it. Jesus was subtly teaching that the will of God is not just your ability to push to a thing, but to push through to a thing.

God gives each of us the capacity to live with a new burst of energy after having run out of breath. We all know the feeling of running out of breath. I do not mean just literally but across a broad spectrum that includes work life, home life, and cultural realities. It is when you just feel like your energy is zapped, knowing that the rest of the race is in itself fatiguing! For the runner, when they hit this wall, if they keep running then there is this passageway into new energy. This is called the "second wind". You start breathing freely again after having been out of breath.

The Spirit becomes your breath on the other side of pushing through life when you feel like you have run out of breath. What it requires though is that you do not quit when "breathless." The second wind can greet you on the other side of the push, but the push is the choice *you* have to make.

Jesus subtly says the same thing in our focal passage. Jesus is teaching the persistence of prayer—that we ought to always pray. That means our prayers will not always be met with immediate evidence of results. Our prayers are heard immediately but maybe manifested eventually. Jesus may have the complete answer ready to release and positions it on the other side of the next prayer.

The same holds true for our lives in general. I want you to develop a spiritual mindset that stops believing that God is responsible for your push. He can incentivize and encourage it. "Run your race with patience, looking to Jesus," and "They that wait upon the Lord shall renew their strength" are motivating and encouraging truths. The push represents the distance between the first wind and the second wind is all yours.

Can you decide to keep showing up, to keep praying, to dry your tears, and present yourself under the pressure again? To feel the fatigue but not quit. To see the distance you have come, not see the destination close enough yet, and nonetheless push through until that second wind comes? This is what Jesus expects of us. I want to tell you that you have a second wind in you. I need you to pray, worship, study, and virtue through to it because the breathing frees up on the other side of the push. You will feel fresh and become capable of operating as if you had not felt the fatigue in the first place.

You have a second wind in you, but you will never know it if you do not push past the fatigue of the first wind. When the body endures ten to fifteen minutes of running through the fatigue to find its second wind, it is because the body stops pushing out carbon dioxide and starts taking in oxygen. Now, do not focus on the carbon dioxide part or the oxygen part; that is out of my field of expertise. I could not explain all of the chemistry if I tried. Instead, focus on the ten to fifteen minutes that the body uses to make the switch from expulsion to intake. The pass through the wall takes place because the body stops worrying about what it is losing and start focusing on what it needs to take in.

The stressors and challenges you live with every day—the constant expulsion of always giving out, showing up, and needing to perform—are exhausting. God has a second wind of provision, grace, and blessing waiting for you on the other side of a small window in between. That requires of you one choice. Can you not become a prisoner of all that you give out and spend your energy on what you need to take in to live in that small window until your second wind kicks into gear?

How long do you need to pray? How much more Scripture do you need to meditate on? Who do you need to spend time with? What space in your week's calendar can you carve out for solitude? Make the switch and decide to not focus on how much still has to be done while being this tired already; instead, focus on what you need to intake to help get you through the small in-between time until God lets your second wind kick into gear. In Luke, Jesus says it is persistent prayer. The writer of Ecclesiastes says it is endurance. Scripture also teaches that it is patience and sacrifice. All of these are ways of taking into your spirit what is necessary to walk short of breath until that second wind kicks into gear.

And it will kick into gear.

> **There is a story of a weak and sickly man. The man was sick but could not afford to go to the town doctor. The man lived in the deep backwoods in an old log cabin. His condition seemed to grow worse by the day.**

> **Out in front of his cabin was a huge boulder. The rock was massive. One night in a vision, God told the sickly man to go out and push the huge rock all day long, day after day. The man got up early in the morning and with great excitement, he pushed the rock until lunch, then he rested a while and pushed the rock until supper time. The man loved pushing against the rock; it gave him meaning. The dream was so real that it was with great excitement that he pushed against the rock.**

Day after day, he pushed. The day rolled into week and week into months. The sickly man faithfully pushed against the rock.

After eight months of pushing the rock, the weak sickly man was getting tired of pushing the rock so much. In his tiredness, the man started to doubt his dream. One day, he measured from his porch to the rock, so that he could check his progress over time. After four more weeks of pushing and measuring, the man realized he had not moved the boulder even a fraction of an inch. The boulder was in the same place as when he started.

The man was disappointed. He had thought the dream was special. Now after nine months, the sickly man saw that his work had accomplished nothing. He was tired and his dream seemingly dashed upon the rock. The man sat on his porch, cried, and cried. He had invested many hundreds of hours into nothing. Nothing! It was all for nothing!

As the sun was setting in the west, Jesus came and sat down next to the man as he cried. Jesus said, "Son, why are you crying?"

The man replied, "Lord, You know how sick and weak I am. Then, this dumb dream gave me false hope. I have pushed with all that was within me for over nine months, and that dumb old rock is right where it was when I started."

Jesus was kind and said to him, "I never told you to move the rock. I told you to push against the rock."

The man replied, "Yes, Sir, that was the dream."

Jesus told the man to step in front of the mirror and look at himself. As an act of obedience, the man stepped in front of a mirror and looked at himself. The man was amazed. He had been sickly and weak, but what he saw in the mirror was a strong, muscular man. The man realized that he had not been coughing all night. The man started thinking of how well he felt for several months. The man considered the strength that he had built by pushing on the rock. Then the man realized that the plan of God was not for the rock, but him.

The push towards the second wind is not about the race; it is about you as the runner. It always has been and always will be.

QUESTIONS FOR THOUGHT

1. Are you feeling like you are spiritually, emotionally, or mentally "out of breath"?

2. What motivation do you have to push forward despite your fatigue?

3. Have you ever been asked to "push on a rock," where you did not understand the purpose of what you were going through, but the result was a stronger you?

LET US PRAY

Lord, my prayer is simply that You continue to grow us in ways that are best for us. At times it is uncomfortable, requiring that we push past fatigue and frustration, and into that second wind space where we can affirm that perfect peace that surpasses all understanding. Thank You for the confidence You have in us. We want to live with that same confidence in ourselves. We covenant to push and persist, to wait and to hope, knowing that You will bless us with second-wind power on the other side of our push. In Jesus' name, we pray. Amen.

DAY 28 MEDITATION

JOURNALING YOUR JOURNEY

Today, spend time in prayer and reflection on what you have digested in this week's meditations. Record your thoughts, emotions, insights, and prayers on the following pages. "Journaling your journey" through this difficult time in your life not only serves to help you process your experience at the moment but will be something you can look back on in the future as evidence of how God has worked in your life.

_____

_____

_____

_____

Day 28 Meditation: Journaling Your Journey

_____

_____

_____

_____

_____

_____

_____

_____

_____

_____

_____

_____

Day 28 Meditation: Journaling Your Journey

_____

_____

_____

_____

_____

_____

_____

_____

_____

_____

DAY 29 MEDITATION

PERSISTENCE IN YOUR FAITH

American poet Robert Frost is right when he says, "The best way out is always through."

That is how Daniel felt as an exile in Babylon when he, among other young men, was picked from among the slaves to enter the palace as personal servants of the king.

Israel was in one of those low periods when the foe from the north had been successful in penetrating the hedge of protection that comes from walking in covenant obedience with God. The hedge of protection was softened when Israel became filled with self-interest. As a result, the foe from the north defeated Israel and carted off the people of God into bondage. The conquering king wanted to have his attendants find some young men from among the exiles to serve him in the palace and to have the memory of their native culture erased by teaching them the ways of the Chaldeans. Daniel was chosen, among others.

Conflict immediately arose when those who were shaping these boys for a lifetime of servitude were given food to eat, which for Daniel was a violation of the diet that helped him to stay consecrated to his God. Daniel cannot help but test his convictions. Daniel raised an objection which was met with a blanket denial: "You won't have us getting in trouble because you are looking sickly and skinny. You'd better eat this food". Here was Daniel's response:

> **Please test your servants for ten days: Give us nothing but vegetables to eat and water to drink. Then compare our appearance with that of the young men who eat the royal food, and treat your servants in accordance with what you see." (Daniel 1:12-13).**

After this time, Daniel looked healthier and had more energy. Daniel gained respect and established his leadership quality. It is impressive that Daniel decided that no matter the consequences—in a real sense, with no leverage to stand on—he, a servant from among enslaved people in a foreign land, to stand his ground to protect his spiritual commitments. Daniel does this not knowing the consequences, among them the possibility of being killed. Was it Daniel's youth that made him like that? Was it a lack of familiarity with the rules of exile? Was it that nobody told Daniel that he had no voice? Or, was it that he exercised what we all should when pressed to accept anything that will change our spiritual commitments or interfere with our covenant relationship with God? Daniel was persistent.

Hebrew thought would explain it this way: it is making the decision that you will do regularly what you do, no matter what. Daniel was persistent about his commitment to honor God. Daniel could not change it even when choices were taken from him. Now that is a powerful statement.

Something inside of Daniel would not die and could not be suppressed. For him, no stress or pressure could make him abandon his core beliefs. Daniel persisted with skillful resistance. Daniel seemed to say "Let me eat my diet for 10 days and then you check to see if I don't look healthier. I will get as much work done, if not more than, the others". It proved itself in his life. God protected Daniel from the lion he was locked away with.

Your current season of struggle probably feels like Babylon did for Daniel—asking you to give up everything. God wants from us what He rewarded when Daniel displayed it: persistence!

Don't you give up what you believe about God and how you live out that belief. Don't let the demands for your adjustments, patience, and compliance make you soften your convictions, create a crack in your character, or mess up your ability to be who you are spiritually. What has to be paid close attention to is your persistence. Can you keep doing what you do regularly because it is important to not let a season break you? That is the question I raise for you.

If my word carries any weight in your life, then I want you to hear me say that you have what it takes to keep being persistent—to keep leaning on the substance of things hoped for and on the evidence of what is not seen.

Keep feeding your emotions the conviction you carry that makes you trust God. What is that conviction? It is God's imagination working for your good through all of this. You must trust Him enough to stand on your conviction. Don't let the things happening make you crowd the expense on your emotions. Everything is stressed around you, but do not forget to sift these things so they do not cause you to be overwhelmed. If you do not sift them and apply wisdom to tell yourself the truth, then the frustration, regret, anger, hurt, and pain can leave you feeling overwhelmed.

God's expectation is not that you withdraw, not that you develop an attitude about everything, not that you feel frustrated and tense, and cynical about everything. What God wants is for you to give Him an offering of persistence.

Over a synagogue is a light that is called the "always candle" that symbolizes the persistent presence of God, which Jesus put words to when He said, "I will be with you always." Just as God always shines the light of His presence in our lives, we want to respond by always being consistent and regular about who we are in Him.

Let's check in with Daniel and the others to see what their persistence evidenced:

> **So he agreed to this and tested them for ten days. At the end of the ten days they looked healthier and better nourished than any of the young men who ate the royal food. So the guard took away their choice food and the wine they were to drink and gave them vegetables instead. (Daniel 1:14-16).**

Day 29 Meditation: Persistence in Your Faith

This is why James Michener says that "character consists of what you do on the third and fourth tries!"

Listen to the sound of resilience. I love how Job expresses it, which is what I pray for you.

My spirit is broken,

my days are cut short,

the grave awaits me.

Surely mockers surround me;

my eyes must dwell on their hostility.

Give me, O God, the pledge you demand.

Who else will put up security for me?

You have closed their minds to understanding;

therefore you will not let them triumph.

If anyone denounces their friends for reward,

the eyes of their children will fail.

God has made me a byword to everyone,

a man in whose face people spit.

My eyes have grown dim with grief;

my whole frame is but a shadow.

The upright are appalled at this;

the innocent are aroused against the ungodly.

Nevertheless, the righteous will hold to their ways,

and those with clean hands will grow stronger. Job 17:1-9.

Did you hear it? I am not at all minimizing anything in your life. I want to remind you that you have what it takes to stay steady, to be consistent, to get things done, to excel, and to conquer. Expect no less because your testimony is the same as Job's.

QUESTIONS FOR THOUGHT

1. What would persistence look like in your current circumstances?

2. Are you ready to commit today to not let this season break you?

3. Why do you think God values persistence?

LET US PRAY

Lord, I pray that as we shape these days and months to come, no matter our conditions and circumstances. We want to express our confidence and boldness in You through our resilience. We will not give up our joy or sense of well-being because of the upside-down reality we are living with. You have brought us too far and been way too good for us to do that. Continue to convict us around the area of our spiritual resiliency. We intend to prove that we, like Daniel, will not let our trial make us abandon how we live by faith. We love You and want to honor You in all we say and do. In Jesus' name, we pray. Amen.

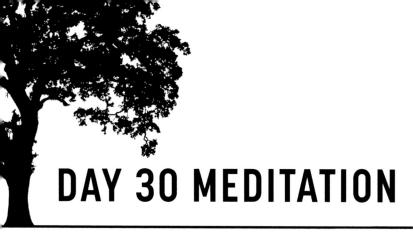

DAY 30 MEDITATION

BAD HABIT? GOOD HABIT? YOU MAKE THE CHOICE!

What is your bad habit? Warren Buffet said, "Chains of habit are too light to be felt until they are too heavy to be broken." An anonymous writer wrote, "Bad habits are easier to abandon today than tomorrow."

I want to spend today focusing on internal spiritual construction projects. I suspect that every one of us battles this: how do I change bad habits? Habits that are centralized in our thinking. Perhaps, when our default thinking is negative or too hard on ourselves, too critical of others, too suspicious, or too vulnerable. Habits are centralized in our actions when we keep envisioning what we fail to ever actually start or dive into. Habits are centralized in our spirituality, when we let God bless but not lead, bestow but not place expectations for how He wants us to steward what He bestows upon us. We know habits are counterproductive. As much as we are loyal to habits, we also know that our future cannot move in kingdom-size progression if we do not break these bad habits.

Paul knew Corinth needed this teaching. In this seaport city where soldiers anticipated having nothing but exhilarating fun and where there was a worship of several gods, a remnant of Christians had been nurtured whom Paul felt responsible for equipping. Paul wanted to equip them to live lives honoring God. Among the many theological topics he hit, Paul gave instructions regarding how to break bad habits! Listen to his words:

> **No temptation has overtaken you except what is common to mankind. And God is faithful; he will not let you be tempted beyond what you can bear. But when you are tempted, he will also provide a way out so that you can endure it. (I Corinthians 10:13).**

"Tempt" in Greek means "test" or "trial." The enemy tempts you around vulnerable openings in your life. He is not into being wrong about what makes you bend or break. He wants to kill, steal, and destroy. Satan does not want to waste time, so he is interested in luring you away from living in the will of God. Satan's first angle of attack is always going to be in the areas of your already-formed bad habits.

Paul says, do not deny that you cannot be wounded because of hits against your habits. It is common to humans and is dangerous to live thinking you are above them. If your habit is to cut corners on your job and to complete assignments but never give them your best, or choosing speed versus quality, or completion versus integrity, then what will the enemy do? The enemy will wait for you, feel the middle ground between these realities, and then like the serpent in the wilderness, he will slither up to your life and squeeze your habits. You may not think it is a problem because you are promoted and compensated despite it. There is coming an opportunity or possibility that will require your habits to be more mature than I have described. It will tell on you—and perhaps cost you–the things you are chasing.

If your habits include letting people slide concerning how they treat you, then the enemy will make sure that a person who can damage you emotionally gets inside your habit. Next time when you are forced to choose between making the demand to be dealt with a certain way or allowing the person to mistreat you again, you will not allow it. By protecting yourself, you will avoid years of trying to repair the damage. Do you get the point?

Don't think you are the exception or that bad habits will not injure you like they do others. Instead, accept that habits are common to men. We all battle bad habits. We all are made to suffer because of bad habits. The good news is, we all can overcome bad habits. It starts by affirming this: God knows you need to change them and He is actively engaged in providing you an opportunity to do so. How? He demonstrates His faithfulness by not letting anything pull on your habits where there is not a choice, a better option, or a way of escape. Isn't that good news? It means you are not going to live forever as a prisoner or a victim of the bad habits that are preventing you from living God's best for you.

So start living like breaking these habits matters! They are as much a priority as discovering the power of your gifts, chasing blessings, and offering praise. As much as I want all that God has for me, I also want to break every bad habit in my life. The good news is that God wants me to break them and provides everything I need to break them when I decide it is the time!

I want you to also affirm that you are stronger than your habits. We know that because Paul says God will provide a way of escape or He will help you to stand up in them, which means He can make you stronger than your habits. Don't live like a slave to bad habits. Stop telling yourself that you cannot change bad habits because you can. Stop giving your habits control. Your habits do not have to control you. You are not weak in your bad habits. You can change sleeping patterns, work out, save money, create new disciplines, your tiredness, schedule, and need for attachment are not masters; they are servants. I hope that you hear me. Not one habit in your life is a master over your life; they are all servants and their master is you!

You either feed your habits or starve them. You give them place and priority or decide to stop them and to take the power away. You make the choice that you want better and different. You are not bowing at bad habit altar anymore.

I want you to affirm one more thing: you deserve to test a life free of these habits. That is what I had to become convicted about: I deserve to live my life in the fullness of God's presence and blessings in my life. If I do not affirm God's presence and blessings in my life, then I will never get motivated to start doing something about them. You deserve to feel what it is like to be led by the Spirit in such a way that life becomes a series of ordered steps. You deserve to be in relationships with people that respect your voice and with whom you can be authentically you. You deserve to work in an environment where you do not have to keep paying tithes to bad habits. I want you to acknowledge that you have bad habits. Then, decide that God made you bigger than them. Remember that a change in habits is a change in life.

A wise old tutor was once taking a stroll through a forest with a curious youth. The tutor suddenly stopped and pointed to four plants close by. The first was a tiny sprout, just coming out of the Earth. The second had rooted itself quite firmly in the fertile soil. The third was in a small shrub. The fourth had grown into a well-developed tree. The teacher said to his young student, "Pull up the first plant." The youth pulled it up easily with his fingers.

"Now pull up the second." The boy obeyed, and with a slight effort the plant came up, root and all. "And now the third." The boy pulled with one hand, then the other, but it would not come. Then he took both hands, and the plant yielded to all his strength.

"And now," said the teacher, "try the fourth." The youth grasped the trunk with all his might, but hardly a leaf shook. "I cannot move it," he said.

"Just so, my son, with all our bad habits. When they are young and small, we can cast them out, but when they are full-grown, they cannot be uprooted."

You may have habits in all four conditions, but not one of them is too rooted that God cannot give you the strength to uproot them. You have no habit that God cannot help you get rid of. Not one. How does hearing that change how you think about what you need to do with them? How does hearing that change when you are going to get started? How does hearing that makes you eager to get started?

With all that God has in store for you, with all that you mean to the body of Christ, and with the ways God wants to use you to bless, inspire, and help someone else's life, do not let a habit, or habits, prevent you from living your best God-intended life.

Day 30 Meditation: Bad Habit? Good Habit?
You Make the Choice!

We all experience times of testing, which is normal for every human being. But God will be faithful to you. He will screen and filter the severity, nature, and timing of every test or trial you face so that you can bear it. And each test is an opportunity to trust him more, for along with every trial God has provided for you a way of escape that will bring you out of it victoriously. (I Corinthians 10:13 TPT).

QUESTIONS FOR THOUGHT

1. What are some bad habits that you feel have grown so big they are impossible for you to remove on your own?

2. Has your current time of hardship, pain, or waiting changed your habits in any way?

3. Does hearing that there is not one habit that God cannot help you change motivate you to act now?

LET US PRAY

Lord, we establish a covenant with You that today we are going to focus on our habits: owning that we have them, accepting what they have meant to us, demystifying their strength and power, replacing them with habits that honor You and that position us for our best lives to be enjoyed and impacted by us and others. Help us to face that we are no different one from another and we all have these nagging habits that we wish we had never developed. We thank You that Your grace is sufficient for us, and we do not have to let these habits master us. We can make them our slaves and eradicate them. Give us deep discernment and ironclad determination. Help us not to wait but to get started immediately.

Make it a great day of spiritual awakening, enlightenment, renewed energy, and hope. We will not let our formed habits root stronger in us than Your Spirit's rooting in our lives. We affirm again that greater are You in us than he that is in this world. Thank You, Jesus, because the victory is ours already. We are excited about what our new habits are going to yield for us, for You, and the expansion of Your kingdom on the Earth. In Jesus' name, we pray. Amen.

DAY 31 MEDITATION

DEVELOPING GOOD HABITS

Science has concluded that it takes between two to eight months to form or break a habit. How long it takes depends on what habit is being formed or broken. Your habits form your life, which is why Jesus does not call salvation an insertion into your life but a conversion. When a person comes to Jesus, they become a new creature, old habits pass away, and new habits are formed. I believe that we go through conversions repetitively: we convert to new and deeper truths and deeper levels of intimacy with the Lord.

Jesus taught in Luke chapter 9 about what it takes to be His disciple. He wants radical faith in Him. Jesus wants total commitment. He wants unswerving loyalty. Jesus wants you to stop protecting bad habits. What makes breaking bad habits so hard sometimes is that we can protect them so long that we cannot imagine life without them.

Listen to Luke 9:61-62:

> **Still another said, "I will follow you, Lord; but first let me go back and say goodbye to my family." Jesus replied, "No one who puts a hand to the plow and looks back is fit for service in the kingdom of God."**

The Message translation says it this way:

> **Then another said, "I'm ready to follow you, Master, but first excuse me while I get things straightened out at home." Jesus said, "No procrastination. No backward looks. You can't put God's kingdom off till tomorrow. Seize the day."**

That woman Jesus met at the well in Sychar was so loyal to her habits that Jesus had to hang them out in front of her before she could surrender to accepting salvation. She submits to breaking the habit and runs back to town, announcing Jesus' gift of salvation in her life.

Today, I want to give you the next layer of breaking bad habits. It is the one that leads all others. Stop protecting bad habits!

Examples: I only eat poorly because of my schedule. I only work all the time because others will not. I am always tired because there is so much to do. If others would, then I could.

You know that we could spend all day naming one thing after another when the truth is, if we stopped protecting bad habits, then we could create different mindsets, passions, scheduling, accountabilities, and thank God, results.

Stop protecting bad habits. Stop accepting bad habits and creating comfortable places for them. Let Jesus confront bad habits as He does the man who asked to go straighten out things at home. These habits the man had formed have found a comfortable hiding place in what appears to be a family-first motif.

We know that Jesus was not being anti-family. Rather, Jesus was unapologetically being kingdom-first. So much so that Jesus says on another occasion that He is setting family members against family members when the kingdom is the issue that separates. Seek first the kingdom!

Let's say you are sitting at your desk. You are angry that you feel so tired. When you get off work you will not have any energy to enjoy any portion of a nice day. A coworker comes by and asks what you intend to do. "I never have time to do anything," you answer. "I've got to go home and do this and that. I am so tired and there is always something to do. My phone is always ringing. Somebody always needs something."

Well, what would happen if you stopped protecting bad habits? You would set your voicemail like this: "Thank you for calling. I will be checking messages between three and four today and returning calls between four and five. If I am not able to return your call today, then I will make every attempt to return your call tomorrow morning between eight and nine.

You would set a television time and watch the shows you recorded. You would do your thinking work at the best time of day for your brain productivity. You would watch or work with a start time and cutoff time. More important than anything else, you would steward your time and not just surrender to your time.

What do I mean by that? Time is a gift God has given you. You can let life lead with respect to your time or you can steward the time and discern how it can make you more of an instrument in God's hands to be used for His glory.

I like music but do not love it like others. I return calls in the car when I am still and cannot be distracted. I learned early on that trying to write my sermon in my church office during the day does not work for me. In my office, there are too many distractions and phone calls. So I shape my sleep to be able to get up early and write. I know my habits when it comes to delayed gratification. If I want to enjoy what I want to do, then I cannot have what I must do on my mind. I do it to the best of my ability the first time so it does not come back around.

This lesson can be translated to so many areas of your life. I know that you might be talking yourself out of addressing the habits that you know apply to this topic. This word is amplified in your head right now: "But..."

Today, just ignore that voice for one minute and replace it with this: "What if...?" What if you stopped protecting that habit and started thinking about what it will take to get it done?

I challenge mentees when they say this: "I wish I had time!" I cut that right off and say, "You do. You have been given a lifetime. Now how are you dividing it?"

What have you let impose upon your time that makes you think you do not have enough of it? I am not saying become robotic and so scheduled that you cannot be spontaneous. I am saying that you need to be intentional and see your habits as a stewardship issue. For God's sake, stop being loyal to bad habits.

There is a book that radically changed my life. It is a book that changed how I do my time, schedule, and people interaction. It is entitled *The Four-Hour Workweek*. In it, the author, Timothy Ferriss, says that today's culture mistakenly values hard work over clever effectiveness. Ferriss gives examples and demonstrates that working a small number of hours on the parts that matter–the 20% that yields 80% of results–are far wiser and more sustainable than working a large number of hours for a slightly higher yield. Ferriss encourages people to ignore social expectations to become well-rounded and focus on multiplying their strengths instead of fixing their weaknesses. In short, Ferriss gives some pretty unorthodox advice. It is most effective because of its unorthodox nature.

It is not what you do longer that necessarily makes something successful. It is when you do it and know when to stop. This is where I get my phone practices. I only return phone calls at a time of day when I am most alert to give the best advice and will not feel the most pull. I only write when I can keep my flow, not be interrupted, and my spirit and brain are optimal. I have a definite cutoff because there is nothing I can produce of quality after a certain time in the day—it is a waste of time for me to try. I could go on and on.

The point I want to make today is this: you cannot form spiritually beneficial habits until you decide to stop being so loyal to bad ones. Get up from kneeling at the altar of bad habits. Stop trying to convince yourself, and others, that they are that strong or that you are that weak. Walk away from the bad ones so that you can discover habits that will bless your life.

QUESTIONS FOR THOUGHT

1. What practical changes could you put into place to give time for the most important things?

2. What habits do you feel loyal to? Enslaved to?

3. If you "had more time," then what would you accomplish for the Lord?

LET US PRAY

Lord, help us to choose this day whom we will serve when it comes to the habits in our lives. Give us the strength to walk away from habits that are not good for us. We want to honor You with our time as much as we do with our words and worship. You have gifted us with time, and we do not want to take that for granted. We can never get back the time You have blessed us with. We confess that we have often filled precious time with habits and practices that have not allowed us to live our best lives for You. Today we confess these sins and ask that You would forgive us.

We will stop using our fatigue, demands, and responsibilities to be covered for the fact that we have not mastered our time and have often been a slave to it. But today we are acknowledging that our times are in Your hands. You have given us the free will to fill these days. We are determined to honor You with them. We are excited about the challenge, focused on rhythm, rest, work, and Sabbath. We love You not only for how You bless but also for how You correct. Now stir disciplines, arrest emotions, attack excuses, and give strength to mind, body, and spirit. We intend to honor You with fresh habits. In Jesus' name, we pray. Amen.

DAY 32 MEDITATION

HOW TO DISCIPLE HABITS

It is a tense time in Luke chapter 22. Jesus was nearing the time when betrayal, arrest, extreme beating, and crucifixion were in His immediate future. Jesus was led to share one last meal with His disciples. Jesus sent a delegation to secure a room from a distant disciple who will host them in his upper chamber. It will be a dinner at which Jesus will reveal the betrayal that will initiate the downward spiral leading to Calvary and the crucifixion. At this same dinner, a disappointing conversation breaks out among the disciples about who among them is the greatest. Jesus has to again teach them that greatness is defined by servanthood and not leading position or placement, among others.

This dinner had rich symbolism that had to be emotionally hard for Jesus because He lifted a cup of wine and bread that both reflected the sacrifice that was going to be offered to God of His own life for the redemption of humankind. Without this sacrifice, sin would continue to mount up a debt that no human could ever pay and the result would be the spiritual death of humanity. Can you imagine the stress, the emotional drain, the pull of Calvary, the frustration over the late-game fumbles by the disciples, the awareness of the betrayal and suspicion of the pain, the cruelty, and the mistreatment that is about to grip His life? What would Jesus do next after having been immersed in this kind of setting?

Jesus did exactly what any of us would do: He revealed His habits in life. His instinctual habits would be discovered because that is what we all do when so much is squeezing fast and none of it can stop or change the course direction. You have seen or even experienced it—a tough season on top of unexpected demands surrounded by regular responsibilities, anchored by uncertain invasions, and all processed with waning emotional strength.

We all run to our habits: smokers smoke more and drinkers drink a lot. Eaters pull out their feel-good food and the needy make instant phone calls. Gym rats work out more and those who isolate disappear. Workers stay at work longer, even if accomplishing little of significance. Shoppers comb websites and make purchases. The list could go on and on.

Everything I told you was a part of this one dinner setting, where all Jesus could do was follow the patterns He had already set in His life. We read these words: "And He came out and went, as was His habit, to the Mount of Olives; and the disciples followed Him". Luke 22:39.

When Jesus got there, we know He left the disciples, found a quiet place, and prayed. Certainly, praying was central. Prayer connected Jesus to His Father giving Him a chance to rehearse purpose and align Himself with the "plan" for redemption once again. Prayer purged perceptions and pushed out all the noise Jesus had heard and was forced to manage among the disciples. But what got Jesus there was this: "as was His habit." If Jesus had developed any other habits, then we would be reading something different. Jesus was only at the Mount of Olives because it was His custom to be there.

We have spent a couple of meditations identifying bad habits and admitting that we have them. We have prayed about ridding our lives of bad habits and asking God to help us not be so loyal to them. Jesus has taught us that one of the discernments we should have about our lives is: what are our good habits? We will need good habits when days for us are like that night was for Jesus. When you have no adequate time to "figure it out" but are being hit with one thing after another in route to the next big thing, which for Him was arrest and all that followed after. For us, it is whatever that next thing is that will not let you breathe because of everything you have been managing.

Ask the Lord to help you identify what your good habits are. Nurture your good habits with greater awareness of the grace they bring to your life. Whatever your custom or habit, you should do it fifteen minutes after you have left the upper room. What are your good habits? How can you make your good habits more of a default when your day or night is like the night Jesus had before going to the Mount of Olives? I am speaking of promoting good habits that are spiritual—not reflected in head-bowed and knee-bent posture, but always including an intimate connection with God.

When I was on staff at New Psalmist, I was somewhere between the age of seventeen and twenty-two years. I cannot remember which, but I do remember the scene like it was yesterday. Bishop had just discovered that he needed lung surgery. It hit him hard. I had never seen him cry before. The experience shook me to walk by his office and witness him standing by his window peering out at downtown Baltimore crying. I knew not to enter the office. I could discern that he and God were having a tense exchange. I returned to my second-floor office and about thirty minutes later my phone rang. It was Miss Major, the church administrator, on the line. She was like the office mom and keeper of all schedules. She asked if Bishop was in my office. When I answered "no", she said, "I haven't seen him in a while, and I am concerned."

I hung up the phone and grabbed my keys, thinking I might need to drive around downtown and find him. When I started down the stairs, it struck me: I knew exactly where he was. I walked through the extremely narrow shoot that connected the Catholic administration building converted into New Psalmist Baptist Church to the pulpit of the sanctuary where I gave my life to Jesus. There was Bishop on the three-manual Allan organ playing hymns.

How did I know he was there? Because like Jesus at the Mount of Olives, it was His custom when stressed, hurt, angry, or needing a break in the day, to go into the sanctuary and play the organ until he regained strength, worked the issue out in his head, calmed down from a meeting, or received the angle he should take in a sermon. I started early on trying to go out there to tell him that he had a call or that I needed some instruction, but I quickly learned that it was a no-interruption zone. If we needed him at his best then we needed to yield to the habit he defaulted to in times that demanded it.

I also knew where to find one of our church members early on in my pastorate. We kept seeing his car parked in a spot in front of a drug house. We had walked him through several rehab seasons already. When no one knew where to find him after two days of not having seen him, we jumped in the car and went straight to that house. We would beg to go in and get him. Dealers with weapons and inhospitable demeanor let us pass, thank God, and up the stairs we went. Sure enough, there he was, defaulting to his bad habit in his attempt to cope with having lost yet another job.

You will do what is your custom when life forces you to—when the decisions needing to be made are wearing you out and the emotions are all over the place when you cannot find that feeling like you are controlling anything, persuading anything, accomplishing anything, or when you get up from normalcy and start moving you know not where. How do you develop good habits so that we will know exactly where to go to find you?

- Don't default into a habit. Decide which habits you will feed.

- Appreciate the grace of God, that He is willing to meet you there.

- Be a good steward of good habits. In other words, do not corrupt a good habit. It is too important for your survival. Don't turn a prayer room into a closet and then the habit of praying gets replaced with searching for clothes.

- Never interpret your habit as a crutch. It is not a sign of weakness but strength.

Here is what I have learned: I cannot always wait on inspiration, but I can always depend on habits. Good habits will benefit me whether I am inspired or not.

Malcolm Gladwell, who is one of my favorite thinkers, says: "Practice isn't the thing you do once and you're good. It's the thing you do that makes you good."

I want you to pray about God helping you to identify your good habits. When He reveals your good habits to you, feed them so that we can know where your Mount of Olives is because it is your custom to be there.

Gary Keller says, "The trick to success is to choose the right habit and bring just enough discipline to establish it."

QUESTIONS FOR THOUGHT

1. Identify some of your good habits. How can you feed those habits?

2. Where is your default place, your Mount of Olives, when things get stressful?

3. Do you ever view your habits as a crutch? As a sign of weakness?

LET US PRAY

Lord, we have prayed about our bad habits and sought to sacrifice them on the altar. Today we ask You to strengthen our good ones. We want our inclination in hard times to be a habitual run to that place, space, and emotion that keeps us in the very center of Your will.

Like Jesus experienced that night, many of our days are filled with the stresses, noises, and demands that are placed upon life. When we fatigue from doing what we have to do and go the way of our habits, may we have developed healthy ones that drive us straight to You.

I pray that You would help us identify our good habits. I pray that we would nurture them in such a way that without much thinking or consideration, we would be found with You in our customary place, ordering our lives, listening to Your voice, seeing Your will, and meditating on Your word. Break bad habits today in our lives and reward good ones with a clear manifestation of Your presence. Thank You for giving us the grace to meet us in our habitual places, and giving us the blessed assurance that You are with us always, even to the end of the age. We love You today and always. In Jesus' name, we pray. Amen.

DAY 33 MEDITATION

SOWING GENEROUSLY TO YOUR GOOD HABITS

Take a short theological trip with me to see why it is important that you give attention to the habits in your life.

What makes us believe every word God says and that every promise in Scripture can be trusted is because of what we believe is the "immutability of God?" It is the belief that God has not changed and never will. The theologian Irenaeus says it best: "God is ever the same, equal and unalterable. God does not change His essence, His being, or His knowledge."

Hebrews 13:8 says, "Jesus Christ is the same yesterday and today and forever."

The reason I started the meditation this way is that it is easy to accept the immutability of God when it comes to His steadfast love for us and His justice that defends those of us who live by faith in Him against the accusations of the enemy. God's immutability holds us through seasons of difficulty and uncertainty. But God's immutability can also be frustrating because there are things in your life that you just wish He would bend on, even if slightly.

Each Sunday night I sit at some point in quiet reflection and decide on a text to preach the next week. Once I identify the text, I will ask God to let it work on me while I sleep. I have at times jokingly, of course, said to God, "And if you see fit to make sure that when I rise, a full manuscript of your creation somehow appears on my iPad, I will be most obliged. In Jesus' name. Amen." I literally will chuckle because I already know that it is not going to happen. Why? Because I live out a calling extended to me by a God who is immutable. Since He does not change, I know faith comes by hearing and hearing by the word. How can the congregation hear without a preacher? So, a sermon can be inspired, but it will not live until it is internalized. A sermon can be given to me but cannot be preached until it passes through me. The treasure is in earthen vessels.

I put a sermon together this way because one of God's immutable laws is this:

Do not be deceived: God cannot be mocked. A man reaps what he sows Whoever sows to please their flesh, from the flesh will reap destruction; whoever sows to please the Spirit, from the Spirit will reap eternal life. Let us not become weary in doing good, for at the proper time we will reap a harvest if we do not give up. Therefore, as we have opportunity, let us do good to all people, especially to those who belong to the family of believers. (Galatians 6:7-10).

Now, Paul talked about money and the need for those who support him to plant resources where they desire to see him effective in ministry. I want you to marry our exploration of the immutability of God with the habits we form in our lives so we can make some definite spiritual decisions. If you reap, in terms of your habits from where you have sown, and the only reason you can ever reap a fleshly habit is to have sown seed to the flesh, then can we assume you have been scattering seed through your habits? The theological principles I want you to become convicted about are these:

- You will not develop bad habits and get powerful and productive results from them.

- You cannot sparingly sow to a good habit and reap a huge harvest from it.

- You cannot cross a habit that feeds your flesh with an expectation of spiritual return.

- Good habits are the result of sowing good spiritual seeds consistently and regularly.

There is no doubt someone has said, "But I am the exception." That may be true, yet God is immutable. God will not change what He wills. God gives growth and power to the spirit for our lives because the flesh starts decaying the day it forms and returns to the dust from which it has come. He sows seed to the spirit because flesh and blood cannot inherit the kingdom of God. So, although you are extremely exceptional, God's immutability means bad habits are always going to be the result of sowing seed in non-fertile grounds, and therefore, there can be no expectation of a bountiful harvest.

How does hearing this change you? It changes me in the sense that I do not want to waste time. If part of my habits include what I do with my time, then I do not want to waste it. I want to sow in fields that are worth the time I am investing. It changes me in the sense that

I do not want to ignore or neglect my spiritual growth. I cannot be so focused on the physical reality that I neglect sowing generously to what produces the best me spiritually. My habits reveal what I am focused on.

Most of almost every day is spent at the job. If you are health conscious, then an hour in the gym. If you are hair conscious, then hours in the shop. Car fanatic? An hour washing the car. Manicure and pedicure? The list goes on. In some of these cases, appointments are necessary.

But for many, these activities are poorly matched by the broken habits of attending church, daily devotions, or merely viewing church. When the need arises, you think: "I gotta get my spirit right before I go have this conversation." When you go to the barn for resources to equip you for this spiritual exchange, there is very little produced. Why? Because you sowed a lot but not to your spirit. Do you get it?

I want you to develop good habits. It starts with a theological conviction: God does not change. I cannot bend or manipulate His will or imagination, so I will only benefit from habits I feed to grow my spiritual health and well-being. Having become convicted about that:

- I will covenant to spend determined time each day with the Lord in devotions. My time with the Lord cannot be altered. I cannot sleep past it, go to bed before it, and eat lunch without it.

- I will ask God to help me discern what habits I need to form that best grow my spirit—from attending church to joining a ministry to sharing my faith with others.

- I will push past a mindset of doing enough and live with a mindset of generous living, including generosity with the seeds I plant in my habits for my spiritual growth.

- I will stop trying to get strong production from scattering seed to my flesh when what I need concerns my spirit.

- I will offer God patience, knowing that the agricultural metaphor means the farmer waits for months before he or she expects to see any movement from seed planted.

Read this account from Luke:

There once was a rich man, expensively dressed in the latest fashions, wasting his days in

conspicuous consumption. A poor man named Lazarus, covered with sores, had been dumped on his doorstep. All he lived for was to get a meal from scraps off the rich man's table. His best friends were the dogs who came and licked his sores.

Then he died, this poor man, and was taken up by the angels to the lap of Abraham. The rich man also died and was buried. In hell and torment, he looked up and saw Abraham in the distance and Lazarus in his lap. He called out, 'Father Abraham, mercy! Have mercy! Send Lazarus to dip his finger in water to cool my tongue. I'm in agony in this fire.'

But Abraham said, 'Child, remember that in your lifetime you got the good things and Lazarus the bad things. It's not like that here. Here he's consoled and you're tormented. Besides, in all these matters there is a huge chasm set between us so that no one can go from us to you even if he wanted to, nor can anyone cross over from you to us.'

The rich man said, 'Then let me ask you, Father: Send him to the house of my father where I have five brothers, so he can tell them the score and warn them so they won't end up here in this place of torment.'

Abraham answered, 'They have Moses and the Prophets to tell them the score. Let them listen to them.'

'I know, Father Abraham,' he said, 'but they're not listening. If someone came back to them from the dead, they would change their ways.'

Abraham replied, 'If they won't listen to Moses and the Prophets, they're not going to be convinced by someone who rises from the dead.' (Luke 16:19-31 MSG).

God does not change. His essence is immutable. His laws are eternal. Sow habits that will reap a huge harvest for you.

QUESTION FOR THOUGHT

1. What spiritual habits have you been sowing too sparingly?

2. What earthly habits have you been sowing too generously?

3. Does knowing that habits are formed slowly, like seeds that grow over time, help you feel better about not having instant success in forming good habits in your life?

LET US PRAY

Lord thank You that You change not. Your love is steadfast, and Your presence is consistently reliable in and for our lives. As we battle these bad habits and build these good habits, help us to feel convicted to sow to the spirit and not to the flesh. So much of our daily exchanges and encounters are earthly, temporal, superficial, and have produced habits that yield more of the same. We want to sow habits that allow us to reap a harvest that makes us more like Your

Son and greater for Your service. Thank You for Your unfailing grace and Your mercies that are new every morning. Thank You that nothing in this life changes You. You are, in fact, the same yesterday, today, and forever. For this, we give You thanks. In Jesus' name, we pray. Amen.

DAY 34 MEDITATION

THE WAY TO AVOID GOING BACK TO BAD HABITS

By the fifth chapter of Galatians, Paul has already defended His apostleship and right to preach the gospel with or without the support of others who were considered human authorities on who is legitimately ranked in the preaching ministry of Jesus. Paul has also defended the gospel itself and the fact that it is by grace alone—apart from human works—that the Christian is freed from the curse of the law and brought into a right relationship with God. So when you start reading chapter 5, Paul has one more point to make—the freedom that a Christian is called into is not a license to live any kind of way. Rather, the Christian has a responsibility to live set apart, holy, and through the power of the Spirit. Paul opened chapter 5 with the one verse that I believe is the most important in the whole epistle. If someone were to ask you what the theme of Galatians is, and what Paul was trying to communicate, then you can direct them quickly to this one verse to pull the entire book together.

> **It is for freedom that Christ has set us free. Stand firm, then, and do not let yourselves be burdened again by a yoke of slavery. (Galatians 5:1).**

The window of biblical interpretation opens wider by simply listening to Scripture in different translations, so here are some others:

> **So stand strong for our freedom! The Anointed One freed us so we wouldn't spend one more day under the yoke of slavery, trapped under the law. (VCE).**

> **Let me be clear, the Anointed One has set us free—not partially, but completely and wonderfully free! We must always cherish this truth and stubbornly refuse to go back into the bondage of our past. (TPT).**

This one verse sums up this whole epistle and our recent exploration of habits. We defined our habits and acknowledged that we all have them—good and bad alike. We confessed that the bad habits needed to be warred against so that we could break them. We confronted our lives about why at times we protect bad habits. We accepted the challenge to stop protecting them. We accepted God's grace that He strengthens us to replace bad habits with good ones. We close out these activities by incarnating this verse and accepting the grace of God to not go back to bad habits.

When the Lord has set you free, Paul says, it is never partially. It is always completely. So the pull on you that your old habits are attempting to make do not have power unless you open your life to them again. The Lord completely set you free from it. Paul has taught us how to not go back to some habits in our lives. How do we not go back?

- Accept that you have not been distanced from them, allowed to breathe from them, or given a chance to rest from them. You have been set free from your bad habits. Their hold has been broken, pull dissipated, and influence diminished. One of the ways you combat thoughts when they rise again is to acknowledge this truth: the Lord set me free from this habit. As an example, you might say, "I don't eat to address my frustrations anymore," "I don't overpromise and underdeliver anymore," "I don't insert myself in others' urgencies until I create for myself issues that were not even mine to begin with," "I don't listen with a rescuer's mind unless led particularly by the Lord," and, "I don't procrastinate with a priority anymore." Why? Because I have been freed from those habits. They no longer have the same hold on me.

- Stubbornly refuse to go back. One of the images this paints for me is "to fight." I have to fight for my freedom. Lingering around your life will be old habits that cost you time, progress, and emotional maturity. These spirits linger because they are hoping you will leave space for them to return. But you do not have to respond. You will have to resist. Paul implies you will also have to fight. Don't get upset when old habits push hard on you; get determined to fight back.

I have spent years fighting one of my bad habits. I do not know when it developed, but it has persisted for years. I had the habit of not celebrating accomplishments between assignments. Something would go well in my life, I would finish an academic program, or reach a professional milestone and my habit was to walk too fast through that small time between what I had completed and what next had to be initiated. I remember graduating from Morgan State but do not remember celebrating it. I remember graduating from Howard but do not remember celebrating it. I remember graduating from United but do not remember celebrating it. I remember presidencies and the honor of having preached on incredible platforms, but I do not remember celebrating them. Three years ago when I turned fifty, it hit me hard that I had reached the halfway point and worked without taking time to enjoy the graces God had peppered in my life.

I had made a promise to myself and a confession to God that I would fight my habit of rushing from one task to the next. It has been a fight to sit down and appreciate something before rushing to whatever is next. Paul says we should stubbornly fight it. Paul adds, "stubbornly", which suggests that you go hard in the fight against old habits. The freedom you have been given by the grace of God is worth fighting for.

What is the one habit that you have surrendered to God, replaced with a good habit, and know that you must fight against? Whatever that habit is, here is how you are going to fight it.

- Refuse to be controlled by anything not Spirit-led in your life.

- Feed where you are going and not where you have been. In other words, spend no time on habits you have surrendered and more time on habits you have developed through Christ.

- Remember that the reason Satan tempts you with old habits is because God's grace to you to replace habits is never partial and always complete. Satan can only hope that you will decide to go backward.

The big challenge is how you will define success when it comes to your habits? Does it have to have elevation attached to it? Remuneration, perhaps? Do you have to be celebrated by people whose approval you seek? Does all the weight have to fall off immediately or does the debt have to be eliminated shortly? You see what I am getting at. The victories in the habits we are talking about are always felt in the inner conversions first.

For the good habits you are creating, measure the blessings with spiritual metrics first. The first success was your conversion to the need to change—your surrender to the Spirit to be moved or stirred, and then the acceptance of the Lord's empowerment to walk it out by faith. So you have already made significant progress. Don't let the habits of others twist your thinking until you start measuring and assessing with blurry vision.

Mother Teresa was attending a party full of dignitaries. The guest list included presidents and statesmen from around the world. They came in their crowns, jewels, and silks. Mother Teresa wore her ever-present sari, which is an everyday garment that has usually been passed down through generations. Hers on that day was held together by a safety pin.

She was engaged in conversation with a nobleman who was intrigued by her work to the poorest of poor in Calcutta. From his vantage point, her work seemed endless and frustrating. He asked her if she ever became discouraged by seeing so few successes.

"No, I do not become discouraged," Mother Teresa answered. "You see, God has not called me to a ministry of success. He has called me to a ministry of mercy."

Her same habits held her everywhere and at all times. Your habits will too if you trust them. Christ has set us free to live a free life. So take your stand! Never again let anyone put a harness of slavery on you.

QUESTIONS FOR THOUGHT

1. Do you truly believe that you have been freed from your bad habits, or do you have a slave's mentality toward them?

2. What does "stubbornly refusing" to go back to old habits look like in your particular case?

3. How will you define success in the development of a good habit?

LET US PRAY

Lord, thank You that we do not have to live in bondage to habits that prevent us from living in the freedom You have secured for us in Your sacrifice on our behalf. We love You for it. We are motivated and inspired to examine our habits and sift those that are Spirit-inspired from those that are not. We thank You that we are not held captive by any thought, imagination, or habit that prevents us from living in the center of Your perfect will. So we have stopped protecting what we know needs to change and we are accepting instead the fight that is before us to develop habits that are pleasing to You. We will put our hands to the plow; we will reach for the prize of the high calling. We thank You and we love You today and always. In Jesus' name, we pray. Amen.

DAY 35 MEDITATION

JOURNALING YOUR JOURNEY

Today, spend time in prayer and reflection on what you have digested in this week's meditations. Record your thoughts, emotions, insights, and prayers on the following pages. "Journaling your journey" through this difficult time in your life not only serves to help you process your experience at the moment but will be something you can look back on in the future as evidence of how God has worked in your life.

_____

_____

_____

_____

Day 35 Meditation: Journaling Your Journey

_____

_____

_____

_____

_____

_____

_____

_____

_____

_____

_____

_____

_____

_____

_____

_____

_____

_____

_____

_____

_____

_____

_____

Day 35 Meditation: Journaling Your Journey

_____

_____

_____

_____

_____

_____

_____

_____

_____

_____

_____

DAY 36 MEDITATION

TRANSFORMING YOURSELF WITH DISCIPLINES

Early in my Christian walk, I was introduced to Richard Foster's *Celebration of Discipline,* a book that invites us to step into the inner world of the spirit. As Jesus did with His disciples, so He invites us to do–to discipline our lives with certain practices that move us from the distractions and noises of this world into the realm of the spirit where we might engage God at deeper levels. Now let me say that "deeper" is not to be confused with a superficial understanding of spirituality when people use the word "deep."

Everything that God is doing in you that has spiritual weight and depth makes you more relatable to people, more enjoyable to be around, more concerned about who lives where in this world, and what rights and privileges we all should have to live—free to show up in the world with the gifts and graces the Lord has given us.

God meets us in the space of our disciplined practices and engages us in the internal transformation that makes us more Christlike in the ways we show up in other places.

I am going to ask you to dedicate a minimum of thirty minutes each day with everything in your life shut down. The phone must go "off." No television, no music, no conversation, no activity you give yourself to the discipline I will introduce you to.

But one comment before we start: don't turn disciplines into law because it will then become drudgery and not an exciting adventure. Don't try to conquer and control it; just explore it. Let the Lord sharpen your focus and guide the exchange. Let's prove to ourselves that we have a depth to our lives we have yet to explore.

- "He [Isaac] went out to the field one evening to meditate, and as he looked up, he saw camels approaching". (Genesis 24:63).

- "On my bed I remember you; I think of you through the watches of the night". (Psalm 63:6).

- "My eyes stay open through the watches of the night, that I may meditate on your promises". (Psalm 119:148).

Meditation is the ability to hear God's voice and obey His Word–no secret words or chants, no mental gymnastics, no special body position, and no flights into cosmic consciousness. Meditation is quieting my life for a time with God, Who desires to fellowship with us. In meditation, the quieting of our lives is to hear God, not for Him to hear us. In meditation, we are growing into what Thomas à Kempis calls "a familiar friendship with Jesus."

We are sinking into the light and life of Christ becoming comfortable with that posture. What happens in meditation is that we create the emotional and spiritual space, which allows Christ to construct an inner sanctuary in the heart.

Revelation 3:20 says, "Here I am! I stand at the door and knock. If anyone hears my voice and opens the door, I will come in and eat with that person, and they with me." I want you to think of meditation as inner fellowship with Jesus. You quiet your life, still all distractions, and He knocks on the door of your heart and mind. You open both to Him. Jesus reveals what makes you more like Him and more obedient to His wants for your life in the world.

Now, do not fall victim to the misconception that Christian and Eastern meditation is the same thing. Eastern meditation is an attempt to empty the mind, while Christian meditation is an attempt to fill the mind. We are not trying to detach but we are trying to attach. Confused? Here is how you can think of it: the detachment from the normal in your life is so that you can have a greater attachment to God. Meditation leads us to the inner wholeness necessary to give ourselves to God freely.

Don't think this is too difficult or complicated. Meditation is not out of touch with reality. Meditation is not psychological manipulation. Meditation is simply a desire to be in fellowship with the Lord. It is descending into one's imagination, which simply gives you a way to prepare to meditate.

- What is the best time for meditation? A time when you can confidently shut yourself off from the world and give yourself to fellowship with God.

- What is the best place for meditation? A place that is quiet and free from interruption.

Prayerfully, you can designate a place that in its setting bids you into meditation.

- What is the best posture for meditation? You can meditate anywhere, anytime, and in any position—remembering that you are searching for a posture that alleviates tension.

Now, let us visit some forms of meditation. Most teachers of meditation would start with central reference points in the Scriptures. Not studying the Scriptures, but internalizing and personalizing them until the written Word becomes the living Word addressed to you. While meditating on Scriptures, you are not focusing on the technical or analytical but on humility. You are just letting the Scriptures sit with you.

Dietrich Bonhoeffer says that just as you do not analyze the words of someone you love but accept them as they are said to you, accept the word of Scripture and ponder it in your heart. Now, remember, you do not enter any passage as a passive bystander but as an active participant. You have a license to go into rooms, walk beside characters, open doors, ask questions, and enter into the conversations.

Another form of meditation is "centering down," which is a time to become still, to enter into the recreating silence, and allow the fragmentation of our minds to become centered. It is paying attention to who you are, how you are breathing, and what you are thinking from surrendering to the silence and stillness.

A third form of meditation is to focus on creation. God can show us His glory through His creation—like the birds in rhythmic conversation that I have recently noticed while walking the hills. I felt like they were talking to each other and sometimes like they were inviting me to the worship they were enjoying.

The fourth form is to meditate on the events of our time and seek to perceive their significance. What we are after is the inner meaning of events—not to gain power but to understand God's perspective concerning events. You cannot meditate on the Passion of Christ and then not meditate on the killings of blacks by white supremacists.

Meditate on the Scriptures, center down in the stillness, let God envelop you in creation, and let God give commentary on the events!

How do you avoid discouragement? Don't seek perfection in the practice but simply explore it. If you fall asleep, then you needed rest more than you needed to meditate. So rest and then meditate when you wake up. Meditation is a lifestyle–not an activity. Don't rush or seek to control it. Give yourself to it slowly, gradually, and let it invite you into deeper levels.

Find thirty minutes each day when you can position yourself in the place you designate for meditation. Start with reading a passage of Scripture and let it draw you in. Don't try to force anything. If it is not coming naturally or easily, then do not get frustrated. Read it again. Sit quietly with it. If your mind wanders, then when it returns, read it again and let it invite you into fellowship with God. Don't look for results. Look at what you see. In other words, any time you give to God, He will make it productive even if the goal was for you to simply pull away.

I have found that many of my discoveries came from spending meditation time wandering around a passage of Scripture until the Lord met me and revealed what He intended or sat with me in fellowship.

I want you to decide which thirty minutes you will give to meditation this week free from distraction, sit in God's presence, and enjoy His fellowship. Remember, what we are after is bigger than spiritual insight and deep revelation. We are after a familiar friendship with God.

QUESTIONS FOR THOUGHT

1. Is it difficult for you to sit still and meditate?

2. Which form of meditation appeals to you most?

3. What do you expect to gain from spending time in meditation?

LET US PRAY

Lord, thank You for inviting us into fellowship with You. With news headlines, instant access to information, the constant communication, our lives are full of disruption. We need to meet You in quiet spaces where our minds can be re-created.

This week, we offer You the exploration of spiritual disciplines and express our gratitude that You enjoy this fellowship with us. We confess that we want a familiar friendship with You. We want to grow deeper in You and more aware of this world in which we live. Bless us this week. May we navigate it in powerful ways, sharing our faith, witnessing to others about Your goodness, and caring for others in compassionate ways. We love You so much today and always. In Jesus' name, we pray. Amen.

DAY 37 MEDITATION

FLASH PRAYERS

Today, we approach the second of the three most common spiritual disciplines: meditation, prayer, and fasting. I am fifty-three years old and have been walking with the Lord since age fifteen. I am still learning what prayer is, including how to give myself to its' mystery and how to make it such a lifestyle that I do not only set aside times to pray but that my life itself is a living experience of prayer. I start each day with a reading meditation of some sort to give focus to my thinking so that my scattered thinking does not have too many things rushing in. If not, then my prayers would be uncontrollable sprays of venting thoughts, never really engaging God around anything that becomes life-transforming for me. After centering my thoughts, I sit in the Scriptures raised by meditations and become the character the text identifies, imagine my reaction to what God said to the character in the text, or think about how to appropriate God's command to the character.

This creates acceptance of the assignment, need for realignment, a conviction about something needing repentance, surrender to a gift that needs sharpening, a way to handle a relationship with someone, and the list goes on.

I start my prayer with my expressed interpretation of how His Word was absorbed by me. Then I make the switch, by asking, "Is this what You intended? What should I glean? What are You saying? How do You want me to appropriate it in my life?" After asking these questions, I will think through my day. I insert this exchange into my day's plans to shape how I can walk with God throughout the entire day.

For example, my devotion this morning was about the prayer nature of Job as opposed to the pious theological prayer performance of most. I thought about the fact that most people today would not want to hear Job pray because he would argue with God, accuse God, express his anger with God, and even at times express his doubts about the goodness of God. How different is that from these polite dances we offer in prayer that result in great performances but little spiritual transformation? The exercise reminded me this morning that I need to find realism again and accept that God wants me to wrestle with His mystery and not ever think I am in a settled place within it. I need to keep wondering why He is leading my life the way that He is. I must be as transparent about that as I can so I can discover new expressions of faith. That was my prayer exchange this morning, which meant today I was having some different kinds of prayer exchanges with God about things that are confusing me about Him. I saw the way people are showing up in this world today. I hope it is helpful to give you a pattern for how to shape an effective devotional session at least with how the prayer in that devotion should look.

Remember what James 4:3 says: "When you ask, you do not receive, because you ask with wrong motives, that you may spend what you get on your pleasures."

The invitation is to ask with the right motives that do not bend towards self-occupation. I want you to rehearse when we have finished our meditation today: prayer is my discipline to think God's thoughts after Him, to desire the things He desires, to love the things He loves, to will the things He wills, and progressively to be taught to see things from God's point of view.

If you are like those who think that everything in the world is already set, then for you there is no need to pray. If things cannot be changed, then why pray? But that is not what I believe. I believe that through prayer things can change and so can we. The disciples understood this. The disciples knew that they needed to learn to pray. In Luke 11:1 they asked to be taught to pray. You must start with this same understanding: prayer is a learning process, never perfected and always explored. The other important element is that prayer involves talking but is not prayer until it involves listening. Søren Kierkegaard once said, "A man prayed, and at first thought that prayer was talking. But he became more and more quiet until in the end he realized prayer is listening."

Never complicated, prayers are answered because God's children ask! When we offer God our imagination, as children bring to their daily engagement, we get close to the center of the prayer environment we seek that brings a spiritual transformation. It is that simple—nothing more and nothing deeper.

I was taught early one dimension of the prayer life that I want to teach you today. This one dimension has radically shaped my life. I grew up in church when the length of prayer was equated with power. The old traditional church deacon, before the formal worship experience began, would stand at the front of the church, and get the morning started with a poetic, flowery, and deeply spiritual prayer that had some length and musicality to it. It was stirring and deeply impactful. We all fell victim to thinking that every prayer we prayed from then on should be like that.

Because of our view of prayer, we found reasons not to have time to pray because it required so much. We needed space and time to engage in prayers like the formal ones from my old church. For me, it was Deacon Major Watkins, now deceased, adorned most Sundays in a black suit. When he stood to pray, the first thing he grabbed was his handkerchief from his pocket which let you know it was about to be "on." Deacon Watkins would grab that microphone, clear his throat, and go to work. When he finished, you could see the sweat running down his brow. It was as if he needed to be rehydrated and made to sit down to let his heartbeat return to normalcy. I can still feel the power of the experience now. But our "every day" is not shaped for these extended periods of prayer.

However, I want to introduce you to the discipline of a "flash prayer" developed by Frank Laubach, who learned to shape his life around "seeing anybody as providing an opportunity to pray." To hear anybody in conversation, on the phone, in the hallway–was to pray. Flash prayers are sent to God about people, events, thoughts, and musings. How do these look and sound?

My pastor's pastor was named "Doctor Harold Alphonso Carter, Sr". His preaching resulted in my pastor's conversion. Dr. Carter licensed and ordained my pastor. As God would arrange the years, it would be Dr. Carter who would be one of my doctoral mentors along with Dr. William Augustus Jones. Dr. Carter was a personality larger than normal. He was charisma on super-high octane. Dr. Carter had served with Dr. King in the movement. He could preach, sing, and lead worship until the heavens opened. If you experienced Dr. Carter's ministry gifts, then it was a spiritual experience every time. He was deeply rooted in the prayer tradition of black people and built his mega-ministry in Baltimore, before mega-ministry was even a concept, around the specific discipline of prayer.

My encounters with Dr. Carter included the discipline of the flash prayer. When I would pass him in an airport, it would go something like this:

- "Dr. Curtis, Dr. Curtis, God bless you. Where are you headed?"

- "Dr. Carter, I am headed to Memphis to preach."

- "Oh Brother Curtis, God be praised. It's going to be a wonderful experience. Been there several times myself to minister. Great people, good food, deeply rich worship. God bless you. Let's pray.

- "God our Father, bless dear Brother Curtis as he ministers. Real power, deep worship. Bless his preaching. In Jesus' name. Amen!

- "OK, Brother Curtis. God bless you. Peace!"

It would last less than two minutes but still impacts my twenty-five-plus years later. Flash prayers are our discipline to practice. You are already spending thirty minutes in meditation each day this week. In addition, throughout the day, I want you to practice the discipline of flash prayers. Every person you come in contact with, close or distant, I want you to mutter under your breath or maybe even aloud if you have a relationship with them. It will not affect your employment status. You should utter a word of prayer. Adjust it for the conditions you find yourself in. With every single person you encounter, physically, over the phone, by text, or email, utter a flash prayer for them. Saturate their lives with the Lord's presence.

What does this do? It keeps you praying, perpetually in a posture of prayer, and all day long. Listen to what Frank Laubach suggests:

> **If thousands of us would experiment with 'swishing prayers' at everyone we meet and would share the results, we could learn a great deal about how to pray including how to pray for others. We could change the whole atmosphere of a nation if thousands of us would constantly throw a cloak of prayer around everyone in our circle of nearness. Units of prayer combined, like drops of water, make an ocean which defies resistance.**

We do not wait to feel like praying. Prayer is like work; we engage it, and at some point, we start to feel it. Prayer takes no time, but if you let it then you will allow it to take up all your time. Thomas Kelly says:

> **There is a way of ordering out mental life on more than one level at once. On one level we may be thinking, discussing, seeing, calculating, meeting all the demands of external affairs. But deep within, behind the scenes, at a profounder**

level, we may also be in prayer and adoration, song and worship, and a gentle receptiveness to divine breathings.

Let's engage the discipline of flash prayers and shape our lives around the desire expressed by Archbishop Tait when he says, "I want a life of greater, deeper, truer prayer."

QUESTIONS FOR THOUGHT

1. What role has prayer played in your current time of difficulty, pain, waiting, or hardship?

2. What would flash prayers serve to accomplish?

3. How much prayer is enough?

LET US PRAY

Lord, teach us to pray! Our lives are made to fellowship with You perpetually and our joy can only be complete when in continual fellowship with You. We want to experience that in our lives—to live each day in Your perpetual expressed presence until every part of every day is You living Your eternal existence through our temporal realities.

Thank You for shaping us to walk with You even while we walk with each other through this human journey. The mystery of Your presence excites our strivings and explorations. You amaze us with Your movements and stir us with Your words. My prayer is that You would bless us in our disciplining of our lives to be living expressions of prayer. In our private and public lives, may our prayers impact and affect others until they are transformed. Bless our day. In Jesus' name, we pray. Amen.

DAY 38 MEDITATION

THE IMPORTANCE OF PROPER FASTING

Fasting is plain and simple. Fasting is abstaining from food for spiritual purposes. A normal fast is to abstain from all food, solid or liquid, but not from water. Jesus was in the wilderness for forty days where He "ate nothing". Towards the end of the forty days, Jesus became "hungry", which implies that He was abstaining from food but not from water. Jesus exemplified a normal fast by abstaining from food for a period of time for spiritual purposes.

A "Daniel fast" or partial fast is a restriction of diet but not total abstention. In Daniel 10, we are told that Daniel fasted only from meat and wine. There are also examples in Scripture of what is called an "absolute fast" when one abstains from both food and water. The implication of an absolute fast is a dire emergency, like

Esther when she learned that execution awaited her people. She instructed Mordecai to tell the Jews to hold a fast—to neither eat nor drink for three days.

So, there are normal fasts, partial fasts, and absolute fasts. I would add that there are also "modified fasts" in which food or water might be replaced with something else. As an example, our modern times would have to include technology, which has become as essential as food and water for many. Fasting from abstaining from the use of technology could bring about the same effect on the body and mind as food and water.

What is essential to remember is that while fasting may be good for the body, great for purging, losing weight, changing habits, and a list of other reasons, the spiritual reason to fast is to become attentive to Scripture. Fasting makes you more aware of God's voice or presence, contemplative about God's will in your life and focused on God's work within you and around you.

Normally, fasting is a private matter between you and God but there is also group fasting. Jesus acknowledges fasting as a regular part of our spiritual lives but makes no specific command concerning it. In Matthew 6:16, He simply says, "when you fast...". Jesus marries fasting to giving and praying. He assumes you will approach it in the same manner that you give to praying, which is consistently and regularly.

I cannot make it any plainer than to suggest that fasting has one purpose. God intends fasting to enhance your spiritually–to focus on Him. The purpose of fasting is God-initiated and God-ordained. Any other purpose must be subservient to it. Physical benefits, success in prayer, receiving power, being given spiritual insight— these things can never replace God being the center and subject of our fasting. This is not to minimize secondary purposes. Never become confused in knowing that they are forever secondary. In Zechariah 7:5, God said:

> **Ask all the people of the land and the priests, 'When you fasted and mourned in the fifth and seventh months for the past seventy years, was it really for me that you fasted?'**

What's the purpose of fasting? To center my life on God. What are some other purposes secondary to that? To have revealed to us the things that control us, such as pride, anger, bitterness, jealousy, strife, and fear. If the things that control are within us, then they will surface during fasting. First, we will rationalize that we are angry because we are hungry. Then, while fasting we will realize that we are angry because the spirit of anger is in us and trust God to deal with it.

Fasting also reminds us that we are sustained by every word that proceeds from the mouth of God. Food does not sustain you but God's Word does.

- But he said to them, "I have food to eat that you know nothing about."

- Then his disciples said to each other, "Could someone have brought him food?"

- "My food," said Jesus, "is to do the will of him who sent me and to finish his work." (John 4:32-34).

Fasting also helps to keep our lives in balance. It is easy to let nonessentials take precedence in our lives— craving things we do not need and neglecting the spiritual essentials we desperately need. Fasting helps to keep things in our lives in their proper perspective.

It is probably best to begin with a partial fast of 24 hours. Begin with fresh fruit juices being added to the water you drink. Do this for your first several fasts. Don't jump out there on a week-long fast or the frustration of the drastic change will overtake the spiritual connection you are seeking with God.

Monitor the inner attitude of the heart. You will be going about your regular day but let the hunger make you pay attention to how you feel about it. When you face these inner attitudes, some will need to be surrendered to God, others mused for their need to mature, and some virtues should be applauded and accepted! The revelation you are looking for from your fasts is how central God is in your life. I like to imagine degrees of closeness, which means when I am engaged in a fast, I ponder these attitudes. I evaluate God's placement in my mind and heart based upon the degrees of the closeness of His voice. Does God sound like He is talking close to my ear, at some distance, or hollering over so many obstacles that I have allowed to be placed between us? I have in seasons experienced all of these and sometimes on the same day.

Listen to how fasting can mature a person. An individual wrote this after committing himself to fast once a week for two years. Notice the progression from the superficial aspects of fasting toward the deeper rewards. The individual remarked:

- I felt a great accomplishment to go a whole day without food. Congratulated me on the fact that I found it so easy.

- I began to see that the above was hardly the goal of fasting. Was helped in this by beginning to feel hungry.

- I began to relate the food fast to other areas of my life where I was more compulsive. I did not need a seat on the bus to be contented.

- I reflected more on Christ's suffering, the suffering of those who are hungry and have hungry babies.

- Six months after beginning the fast discipline, I began to see why two years has been suggested. The experiences change along the way. Hunger on fast days became acute and the temptation to eat stronger. For the first time, I was using the day to find God's will for my life. I began to think about what it meant to surrender one's life.

- I now know that prayer and fasting must be intricately bound together. There is no other way. Yet, that way is not combined with me.

Do you see the progression from self-congratulations to fixed surrender and spiritual insight? He went from being impressed about his ease within the fast and ended with spiritual insight that increased his faith journey as it seeks greater understanding.

Fasting can bring breakthroughs in the spiritual realm that would never happen in any other way. It is a means of God's grace and a blessing that should not be neglected any longer.

We are meditating for thirty minutes every day already. In addition, we are offering flash prayers for every person we contact in whatever way. We add to these, if we are able, a partial fast of twenty-four hours, which constitutes the missing of two meals. By missing two meals we might begin to move our spiritual lives from a focus on self to surrender to God. Pay attention to your focus during the fast. The benefit you are looking for is to position yourself right in the middle of God's purpose for your life. Let all peripheral benefits just fall into place.

QUESTIONS FOR THOUGHT

1. What is the objective of fasting?

2. How do you think fasting might affect your perception of your current circumstances?

3. If you were to undergo a modified fast, what would be a good thing for you to give up for a time?

LET US PRAY

Lord, thank You that You meet us in so many creative ways to bring spiritual purpose to our lives. Thank You that on the other end of our self-denial, there You are, ready to pour into our lives Your purpose, strength, and power. We confess that we get so focused on our strengths, weaknesses, excesses, and needs, that we fail to surrender to the thought that all we truly need is Your life-giving and life-sustaining Word.

We do not want to waste this season we are going through. Please do not let us do that. We want to emerge from this season dripping wet from being submerged in Your purposes. We want to be aware of Your will for us, and we want to meet You in the surrendered spirit in front of every necessary conversion You have ordered, structured, purposed, and planned for our lives. We hunger and thirst for righteousness. Bless our day! Bless our exploration of these disciplines that bring us closer to You. In Jesus' name, we pray. Amen.

DAY 39 MEDITATION

THE DISCIPLINE OF STUDY

Each summer I like to study something that is not theological, although everything studied is "faith seeking to understand" the character and intent of God. I became a student of "the future" because of an August study retreat. I decided to immerse myself in the kinds of cultural disruptions technology was causing. Sitting in airports for twenty-five years and observing the most significant change in human interaction sparked within me a desire to learn about cultural disruptions caused by technology.

I can remember how long the newspaper line used to be in my early years. I remember how loud the conversations shared among people were as they walked and talked in concourses at airports all across the country. I remember when I was struck by the silence in the airport. All I could hear was the noise of floor-shining machinery and the irritating repetition of the announcements to watch our steps on the walking tram. Every so often the silence would be interrupted with an announcement of gate change or a personal item having been left in the security area. But the conversation I remembered hearing from earlier years had disappeared. I realized that the romance we have developed with technology has created such a disruption that we have stopped relating to each other unless a relationship has already been established. I wanted to know why because I needed to understand and reflect on what this disruption means for me as a Christian, a pastor, and a person.

The purpose of the spiritual disciplines is no doubt the transformation of the person. This purpose is seen in the discipline of study. Listen to Paul's words in Philippians 4:8:

> **Finally, brothers and sisters, whatever is true, whatever is noble, whatever is right, whatever is pure, whatever is lovely, whatever is admirable— if anything is excellent or praiseworthy—think about such things.**

Paul meted out this instruction because he wants us to think about these things. He does not say feel them but to study them. We study to shape our "thinking" about things. Study shapes our thinking. What we study directs what we think about.

Our spirituality is no doubt to be felt but you cannot feel your way into holiness, an anointed, purposeful, or impactful spiritual life alone. You must study the truth because John 8:32, says: "Then you will know the truth, and the truth will set you free."

Jesus makes it expressly clear that the knowledge of the truth will make you free. Good feelings and ecstatic experiences, or "getting high on Jesus", will not ultimately free us. It is the knowledge of the truth that will set us free.

What is study? It is giving special attention to reality so that the mind can move in a certain direction. Your mind will always conform and move in the direction of your concentrations. If we study something long enough, then our habits will be ingrained by what we study. If you feed your mind by concentrating for long hours, then you will develop habits around that. Let me suggest that this is why we are saturated with consumer marketing. Could you imagine if every pop-up on your screen and every piece of print media you received advertised saving your money? Where to store your money, how not to spend it, how to make it last, how to multiply it, why it is important to save, who will benefit from it—if these were our concentrations then our habits would follow. But we are instead saturated with the opposite. What to purchase, why we need it, how many places to get it, how many people already have it, and why you better hurry up and get it. We are made to concentrate on these things. Our habits have become ingrained so that we tend to predominantly think about how to spend money, not how to save it or pass it on to succeeding generations.

This is why Deuteronomy 11:18 tells us that Israel was given this instruction: "Fix these words of mine in your hearts and minds; tie them as symbols on your hands and bind them on your foreheads." God wanted to repeatedly direct their minds. God regularly directed Israel toward certain modes of thought about Him and human relationships. In the New Testament, laws written on doorposts are replaced with laws written on the human heart—the place where Jesus becomes our inward Teacher through the presence of the Holy Spirit. What you study will determine the kind of habits you form.

We need meditation to feed our devotional lives. We study to analyze so that we know exactly what to meditate on. What we study is verbal, such as books and lectures, and nonverbal, such as events, experiences, and observations.

There are four suggested steps to the discipline of spiritual study:

1. **Repetition:** Repeating something channels the mind in a specific direction, which ingrains habits of thought. You can change your behavior through repetition.

2. **Concentration:** Focusing attention on what is being studied. When we center our attention on something and avoid distraction, we bring something into the singleness of purpose.

3. **Comprehension:** This focuses attention on the knowledge of the truth. Comprehension is where insight and discernment emerge.

4. **Reflection:** Whereas comprehension defines what we are studying, reflection defines the significance of what we are studying. Reflection is where we start seeing something from God's perspective.

Day 39 Meditation: The Discipline of Study

Studying requires patience because your first step is to understand, followed by interpreting what you are studying, and then evaluating it. As you study Scripture, you cannot read Scripture only to feel and appropriate it. Feeling and appropriating Scripture is not sinning. They do not result in the replacement of habits with ingrained behaviors that make you a strong Christian. The following is a recipe for studying Scripture:

- Pick a verse, a chapter, a book of the Bible, and read it first to understand it. Consider who it was written to, by whom, and for what purpose.

- Then study and analyze the selected Scripture. Look at word structure and placement of thoughts, filtered through how others thought about it. Then, think about it now.

- Next, evaluate it. Consider how the selected reading makes you feel? What does it awaken or challenge in you? How does it affect how you show up in the world?

When I need to form habits around what I have studied, I repeat reading the Scripture, concentrate on it, comprehend it, and spend time reflecting on it.

If you are resonating at all with the need for study in your life, then accept also:

- A spiritual study has to be planned.

- A spiritual study has to be strategic.

- A spiritual study requires discipline.

If we are studying the Bible, then it is because we are attempting to be controlled by the Author.

So what is our practice? Plan to study. Decide a portion of the day. For me, it was deciding to get up earlier than I was accustomed to. You may choose to stay up later, to give up lunch conversation, or to not listen to music in the car and replace that with the Bible on audio. Plan to study. Resist the temptation to go in with the need to feel anything except a hunger to analyze a passage, or passages, and then take your time. Repeat it several times until you can almost recite the selected passage without reading it. Ask yourself these questions:

- Who was it written to and why?

- Who is the author?

- What was the intent of the author?

- How was that intent received?

- What was the result?

- How am I to understand the need for the lesson in my life and where it will be best reflected?

- What do I think of it?

- How do I suspect it might become a habit in my own life?

II Timothy 2:15 says:

Study and do your best to present yourself to God approved, a workman [tested by trial] who has no reason to be ashamed, accurately handling and skillfully teaching the word of truth. (AMP).

QUESTIONS FOR THOUGHT

1. Does the thought of studying during a time of hardship seem cumbersome? If so, then how can you change that perception?

2. What are some things that you have studied in life which have benefited you?

3. When is a practical time you can set aside to study the Bible?

LET US PRAY

Thank You, Lord, for giving us more than a spiritual high, because our habits would take us down repeated wrong paths if it were not for You to give us the capacity to study. We want to know You in the power of Your resurrection and the fellowship of Your suffering. We offer You the discipline of our study. Teach us to live in the ways You have envisioned for us. Show us Your more excellent way. Let our habits become ingrained as influenced by Your word and the urgings of Your Spirit that lives in us. In all our learning, help us to understand, so that knowing the truth, we can live truly free. In Jesus' name, we pray. Amen.

DAY 40 MEDITATION

SEEKING THE KINGDOM FIRST

Read Matthew 6:25-33 (MSG):

> If you decide for God, living a life of God-worship, it follows that you don't fuss about what's on the table at mealtimes or whether the clothes in your closet are in fashion. There is far more to your life than the food you put in your stomach, more to your outer appearance than the clothes you hang on your body. Look at the birds, free and unfettered, not tied down to a job description, careless in the care of God. And you count far more to him than birds.
>
> Has anyone by fussing in front of the mirror ever gotten taller by so much as an inch? All this time and money wasted on fashion—do you think it

makes that much difference? Instead of looking at the fashions, walk out into the fields and look at the wildflowers. They never primp or shop, but have you ever seen color and design quite like it? The ten best-dressed men and women in the country look shabby alongside them.

If God gives such attention to the appearance of wildflowers—most of which are never even seen—don't you think he'll attend to you, take pride in you, do his best for you? What I'm trying to do here is to get you to relax, to not be so preoccupied with *getting,* so you can respond to God's *giving.* People who don't know God and the way he works fuss over these things, but you know both God and how he works. Steep your life in God-reality, God-initiative, God-provisions. Don't worry about missing out. You'll find all your everyday human concerns will be met.

Søren Kierkegaard, whose theological mind most reflects how I think about faith and ministry, considered what sort of effort could be made to pursue the kingdom of God. Should a person get a suitable job to exert a virtuous influence? His answer was "no" believing must first seek God's kingdom. Then should we give away all our money to feed the poor? Again, the answer is no. We must first seek the kingdom. Well then, perhaps we are to go out and preach this truth to the world: that people are to seek first God's kingdom? Once again, the answer is a resounding no. We are first to seek the kingdom of God. Kierkegaard concluded: "Then in a certain sense it is nothing I shall do. Yes, certainly, in a certain sense it is nothing, become nothing before God, learn to keep silent; in this silence is the beginning, which is, first to seek God's kingdom."

The central point for the discipline of simplicity is to seek the kingdom of God and His righteousness, then everything necessary will come in its proper order. This discipline provides the needed perspective which allows us to receive the provision of God as a gift. A gift that is not ours to keep and can be freely shared with others. God denounces both the materialist and the ascetic with equal vigor because the center of simplicity is not about what you have, how much you should have, or how much of what you have you should give away.

Simplicity is finding the center from seeking first the kingdom. Simplicity is where you can truly be content with such things as you have. A spiritual maturity where comparisons are no longer needed. One's identity is not tied up in the abundance of things that they have nor in the lack of things possessed. It is a freedom from the inner vulnerability that comes with upgrades, later models, and recent fashions. Simplicity is the discipline that reorients our lives so that possessions can be enjoyed without destroying us.

One of the ways you can look at simplicity is to think of it this way: God has created my life for me to manage or steward. So much about that management pushes me to a place of anxiety. Simplicity is the fence that borders my life. Where I stay within that border is to live absent of anxiety. Going beyond that border is to experience anxiety, best described as the wolf having entered the sheep pen.

Freedom from anxiety is characterized by three inner attitudes:

- What I have I received as a gift from God.

- What I have is to be cared for by God.

- What I have is available to others.

This is the inward reality of simplicity. If you do not have an inner attitude that reflects this, then you live in anxiety because no one can ever ride in what you drive, sit on your living room furniture, eat out back at your house, mistakenly step on your shoe, spill coffee on your tie, mistakenly touch your hair, set your purse on the floor, or mistakenly drop your golf club.

If we can find the discipline of simplicity, then everything we have is understood as a gift from God and available to God for His purposes in others' lives.

Simplicity is not just an inner reality. It is also an outer expression. The discipline looks like this:

- Purchase things for their usefulness rather than their status. Not having more than is reasonable is the mindset. Ask the Lord to free you from "label" imprisonment.

- Reject anything that is producing an addiction in you. Whatever in your life that you feel you cannot do without is probably where you want to exercise the discipline so that you can gain control of it. You are just attempting to ensure that you do not become a slave to anything.

- Develop a habit of giving things away. If you are becoming attached to something, then consider giving it to someone who needs it. This is the practice of de-accumulation. Don't forget this one.

- Refuse to live being propagandized by the custodians of modernity—the search for the latest—thinking it is best. I fail at this with the iPhone and other Apple products.

- Learn to enjoy things without owning them. Learn to enjoy a place without thinking about how to buy it. I love a certain golf place. I visit my golf heaven every year. Almost every conversation I have described that place results in somebody saying, "You ought to buy a place there." I had not thought about buying there until it was mentioned. After hearing the suggestion, it took a lot for me to stop thinking about buying because I became gripped by the anxiety of trying to figure out how to. Just learn to enjoy things without having to own them.

- Develop a deeper appreciation for the Creation—get closer to the Earth by walking around whenever you can. Until the pandemic, I never noticed the musicality and chattiness of birds. But the daily walking around my neighborhood has amplified this in my life.

- Look with a healthy skepticism at all "buy now, pay later" schemes. Think of interest as a tool and not an escape. If you cannot use interest to your advantage but need it for your purchase, then opt-out.

- Practice plain honest speech. Avoid both flattery and half-truths. Simple honesty and integrity are best.

- Reject anything that breeds the oppression of others. Where we purchase and what we purchase is critical.

- Shun anything that distracts you from seeking first the kingdom of God. Check your pursuits to ensure that you are not being pulled in so many directions that you cannot determine whether any of them are in pursuit of the kingdom.

I want you to find something of importance to you. Hold it. Touch it. Pray a prayer of gratitude that God trusted you with it and then ask Him to reveal who you should give it away to. Pray that it spiritually impacts their lives and then thank God that in the way you received it, now you freely give it away. Close your prayer asking God to renew your spirit by it, so that you can live free from anxiety and free to seek first His kingdom.

Afterward, spend the rest of the day thinking about ways you might simplify your life only as you seek His kingdom. I was embarrassingly transformed in the pandemic season when I realized how much more effective I was in ministry with so much less busyness. I have repented of equating fatigue with sacrifice. I have had to admit to the Lord that I wanted my fatigue to be weighed heavy and equated with devotion. The pandemic season taught me that my devotion is my devotion while my rhythm and flow are best when in pursuit of the kingdom.

The discipline of simplicity invites us to secure again those borders that keep us from wandering too far into the field of anxiety.

QUESTIONS FOR THOUGHT

1. What does simplicity allow you to focus more attention and time on?

2. Which of the ten tips above have you felt most convicted of?

3. What are other ways that you can simplify your life?

LET US PRAY

Lord, help us to simplify our lives as we pursue Your kingdom. We know that the blessing is not in the simplifying, but the simplifying helps us to be free to pursue Your kingdom. You are so majestic in Your ways and often we have not discerned why You lead us the way that You do, but today we express our gratitude and love You all the more for it. We want to live anxious for nothing and in all things by prayer and supplication make our requests known to You, knowing that the peace You promised us will guard and protect our hearts and minds. We thank You for it, in Jesus' name. Amen.

DAY 41 MEDITATION

MEDITATING AWAY THE EFFECTS OF THE EGO

John 12:24 says:

> **Very truly I tell you, unless a kernel of wheat falls to the ground and dies, it remains only a single seed. But if it dies, it produces many seeds.**

We are focused today on letting go of the self-created images that appease the character expectations that others have of us—and that we fully buy into—which create thoughts and behaviors that protect our need to be accepted and understood.

Paul's revelation that we have died in Christ means we acknowledge in our salvation that we are nothing aside from the primal "I" that constitutes the original intent of God for our lives. It is in this acknowledgment of my nothingness that I am graced and gifted with everything in my life from God. I give up everything my self-created image chases and get everything God's will has for me.

I do not have to chase, protect, defend, and demean. I can love myself and others authentically because I know that I am only what God intended for my life. With this knowledge, I can live with that and be affirmed. The enemy to this is my ego, which desperately needs affirmation, approval, and acceptance. My ego needs to compete and compare because it is always checking its standing in the world. My ego is only satisfied when it confirms superiority compared to others or loathes the reality that I may be inferior when compared to others.

Jesus says that the only way to live your true life free of these kinds of ego-needs is to die in Him. Of course, He does not mean to die. Rather, Jesus means to die to sin and the life it creates. These ego needs are so insatiable that they lead to wanting to be God rather than to want to follow and enjoy Him forever. Jesus explains the process of growing into the freedom of life like a kernel of wheat that falls to the ground and dies. In Jesus' explanation, if wheat does not fall to the ground, then the kernel remains but a single seed.

I want you to think of the kernel as a container. It has so much potential in it but only exists to reach that potential if it dies so that the container can release it. Likewise, if we think in terms of the kernel being your ego or your self-created image which performs to fit norms and compares to find meaning through performance comparisons, then Jesus wants to grace you to walk through the release of that image of yourself. It will feel like death but you can emerge on the other side of it to the nothingness that allows you to be known, accepted, and appreciated for who you are in Christ. It is learning to live trusting the true you. Richard Rohr puts it this way:

> **Our [egoic] self is who we think we are, but our thinking does not make it true. It is a social and mental construct that gets us started on life's journey. It is a set of agreements between us as individuals and our parents, families, school friends, partner or spouse, culture, and religion. It is our 'container.'"**

Let me encourage you to focus on the word "container". The container is largely defined by its distinction from other people. The container is necessary to get started in life but becomes a problem when we stop there and spend the rest of our lives promoting and protecting it. The small and separate self is merely our launching pad, appearance, education, job, money, and success. These are the trappings of ego that help us get through an ordinary day. Don't underestimate how much our culture is container driven.

Let me illustrate this because I meet people who are so container-driven that they miss how content empty they are. I have two Yeti containers: one for cold beverages and one that has never had anything in it but hot green tea. When I am going out for a round of golf, I take them both. I was amazed the other day when I discovered that they both hold the same amount of liquid. They are shaped differently, with one appearing to hold way more than the other. It looks bigger, is shaped in a way that makes you think it doubles the amount of liquid it can house, but the truth is they both hold the same amount.

This is my want for us: that we spend these days doing the painful but beautiful work of the interior spaces in our lives. I want us to die to these container issues that come from a self-created image that makes us live far less than the abundant and complete life that the Lord has envisioned for us.

When we can move beyond our separate selves, it will feel as if we have lost nothing important. Of course, if we do not know that there is anything "beyond" the separate self, then the transition will probably feel like dying. Only after we have fallen into the true self will we be able to say with the mystic named Rumi, "What have I ever lost by dying?" We have discovered true freedom and liberation. When we are connected to the whole of who we are, then we do not need to protect or defend the smaller parts. When we live in a relationship with Jesus like this, it is inexhaustible and we become unhurtable. Your true self cannot be hurt. Why? Because what is said to you or about you is not processed in the ego anymore—it is processed in the life of faith you possess. That faith interprets it in light of the truth of who Jesus says you are. Because you live with the weight being heavier on truth, you do not have to be hurt by the weightless opinions of others. Let me give you a biblical example:

> **When day came, the Council of the elders of the people (Sanhedrin, Jewish High Court) assembled, both chief priests and scribes; and they led Jesus away to the council chamber, saying, "If You are the Christ (the Messiah, the Anointed), tell us." But He said to them, "If I tell you, you will not believe [what I say], and if I ask a question, you will not answer. But from now on, the Son of Man**

will be seated at the right hand of the power of God." And they all said, "Are You the Son of God, then?" He replied, "It is just as you say." Then they asked, "What further need of testimony do we have? For we ourselves have heard it from His own mouth." (Luke 22:66-71 AMP).

For Jesus, there was no need to defend or define because He knew the intent was for them to only destroy the container. Destroying the container would release the redeeming intent of God.

If we do not let go of our separate self, our false self, at the right time and in the right way, then we remain stuck, trapped, and addicted. The original word for this is sin. Trust me, there are a whole lot of people who reach old age still imprisoned to their egoic operating systems. I do not want that for you. I want you to live out of your true self.

Sometime soon, I want you to find quiet time and meditate on who you are aside from your container. Write your reflections and notice how hard it is to even get to it through the demands your container puts on you. What I mean by that is, it will be a struggle to define you without using the words others have used to define you, including parents, coworkers, friends, and family.

Then I want you to strip away what you feel you need to defend, inflate, restrict, and obscure. You cannot create an identity you do not have, so no embellishment is permitted. See what remains after you have stripped these things away because that will be the grace of God—to have met you in the place of nothingness where He can then give and show you everything.

One outcome of the pandemic was that I was introduced to my true self—the self that has no busy schedule and no performance demands, where watches, shoes, crowds, and applause have no place. I thought, "What do I have left?" and God said, "What you have left is the you I have intended all along." I am getting to know myself in ways that were so distant, sporadic, infrequent, and sometimes not genuine. Having spent some time with me that has been offered God's everything—learning to live with the nothingness the container offers—I do not have to win, defend, define, wait for acceptance, affirm assumptions, deflate another to inflate myself, regret not being considered, or get angry about how I was considered. In that space, losses mean something different and victories settle in a different place in my life.

Don't be afraid for the kernel to fall to the ground and die. It is the only way it emerges to an existence unrestricted by its container. Likewise, do not fear the way portions of your life are feeling like a death, because it too is just gracing you to release the container that helps you emerge to the true you that lives in that place where ego has no influence and Jesus defines the meaning of your life.

QUESTIONS FOR THOUGHT

1. Do you define yourself in terms of how others define you?

2. In the battle between ego and true self, how do you ensure that the true self wins?

3. What is a realistic time and place this week that you can set aside to meditate on who you are aside from your container?

LET US PRAY

Lord, help us all to see the value of fighting these egos that You intended to get us started in life but never intended for us to get stuck in. We see their destruction and are fatigued by their demands both in us and around us. Thank You that in faith we can die to our egos. You have blessed us to emerge to the life You originally intended for us—a life so full of meaning and value. Today, we fight the fear, resist the pull of the ego, and we ask You to meet us at the place of surrender because we admit that these container-focused lives we are living are not what you intend for us. We want meaning, substance, essence, and value. To get a life these values, we know we have to die to this self-created life. It is an easy sacrifice because we want the life You've imagined for us.

We are trying to affirm that You have not given us the spirit of fear, but we also confess that this time of personal hardship has us full of angst and nervousness. We trust Your love. It is casting out our fear. We accept that Your Spirit gives us power and creates in us a strong mind. We love You today and we love You always. In Jesus' name, we pray. Amen.

DAY 42 MEDITATION

JOURNALING YOUR JOURNEY

Today, spend time in prayer and reflection on what you have digested in this week's meditations. Record your thoughts, emotions, insights, and prayers on the following pages. "Journaling your journey" through this difficult time in your life not only serves to help you process your experience at the moment but will be something you can look back on in the future as evidence of how God has worked in your life.

_____

_____

_____

_____

Day 42 Meditation: Journaling Your Journey

_____

_____

_____

_____

_____

_____

_____

_____

_____

_____

_____

_____

Day 42 Meditation: Journaling Your Journey

_____

_____

_____

_____

_____

_____

_____

_____

_____

_____

_____

BIOGRAPHY

 At the age of 17, Dr. William H. Curtis accepted the call to ministry. He currently serves as Senior Pastor of the Mount Ararat Baptist Church, a large, urban ministry that ministers to more than 10,000 members in the community. In addition, Dr. Curtis has been an instructor at the United Theological Seminary, and is Co-Owner of The Church Online, LLC, a successful full-service marketing, technology, and publishing company.

Dr. Curtis holds a Bachelor of Arts Degree in Religious Studies and Philosophy from Morgan State University, a Master of Divinity Degree from Howard University School of Divinity, and a Doctor of Ministry Degree from United Theological Seminary in Dayton, Ohio.

He is the author of three other popular books, *Dressed for Victory: Putting on the Full Armor of God*, *Faith: Learning to Live Without Fear*, and *Mentorshift*.

Dr. Curtis is married to Mrs. Christine Curtis, and they are the proud parents of one lovely daughter, Houston.